KILLER
Gators and Crocs

KILLER
Gators and Crocs
Gruesome Encounters from Across the Globe

MICHAEL GARLOCK

THE LYONS PRESS
GUILFORD, CONNECTICUT
AN IMPRINT OF THE GLOBE PEQUOT PRESS

To the memory of John Behler who extended kindness
and consideration to a stranger.

_____

The Lyons Press is an imprint of The Globe Pequot Press.

10 9 8 7 6 5 4 3 2 1

Printed in the United States of America

ISBN-13: 978-1-59228-975-2
ISBN-10: 1-59228-975-4

Library of Congress Cataloging-in-Publication Data is available on file.

CONTENTS

INTRODUCTION

■■ Misfortune has many guises, and if you happen to be living in a temperate part of the world and your luck has run out without your knowing it, calamity may take the form of an opportunistic, ambush-hunting alligator, caiman, or crocodile.

These large reptiles are fully capable of devouring people and they sometimes do just that, with the swish of a tail and a frighteningly fast explosion of energy followed by a bone-crunching bite. If not instantaneous, death soon follows, leaving the crocodilian to consume its meal at leisure.

All crocodilians learned the art of survival millions of years ago. Perfectly adapted to their marine environments, they are happiest when left alone.

Many people, myself included, find them fascinating. Imbued with millennia-old mystique, these modern-day dragons go about their daily business today in much the same ways as they have since the Triassic period of the Mesozoic era, the dawn of the "age of reptiles" approximately 200 million years ago.

Misfortune does indeed wait in the form of crocodilians, but their vertical-slitted eyes are windows that offer tantalizing glimpses of the past, the present, and the future.

CHAPTER ONE

CROCODILIANS: FILM, FACT, FICTION

■ ■ In a perfect world, every animal would be accorded equal value and protection irrespective of size, habitat, physical appearance, or telegenic qualities. By and large, this is a guiding principle followed with varying degrees of success by every federal, state, and local regulating agency in the United States, and, usually with more vigor although not necessarily more success, by animal conservation and rights groups worldwide.

It doesn't matter whether your beliefs or perspective are based on creationism or evolution, because in the moral and intellectual vacuum that altruism often produces, it is at best nigh near impossible (or at worst, a contradiction in terms) to rank life forms in handily quantifiable values. We do not live in a perfect world.

Different—and often diametrically opposed—interest groups are constantly at odds. There are hundreds if not thousands of animal rights groups throughout the United States, ranging from the relatively benign—such as the ASPCA (American Society for the Prevention of Cruelty to Animals)—to the extremely proactive ALF (Animal Liberation

Front). Some groups are small and local; others have a large national constituency. No matter what their annual operating budgets, or their agenda-driven public policies, they are all endeavoring to make right what they believe to be grave moral and ethical injustices.

Some, like Greenpeace and PETA (People for the Ethical Treatment of Animals) gather worldwide attention, while smaller, local groups get little or no press coverage at all. Similarly, certain animals (for disparate reasons) receive more attention or notoriety than others. The spotted owl, the snail darter, and certain species of whales and wolves are usually guaranteed to stir up controversy for a variety of reasons, all of which have been well documented.

A few groups might be labeled "on the cusp of the lunatic fringe," and some larger ones are so big and have so much money that they become almost bogged down in their own bureaucracy. Several animal and/or environmental rights groups have become elitist and almost cultish in their self-righteous zeal to protect the animals from people, and by sometimes not so tacit implication, the people from themselves.

Large organizations such as the Audubon Society, the Sierra Club, and the World Wildlife Fund have annual operating budgets in the millions of dollars. However, most animal rights enterprises do not have the financial clout to hire professional lobbyists whose job it is to put pressure on influential members of Congress, state representatives, and local politicians.

There are also counterparts in the form of different groups who are opposed (again, for a dizzying array of reasons) to the specific aims of certain animal rights groups. Unfortunately, given the nature of the democratic process, even with its obvious faults and hypocrisy, apathy is often the result.

There's a constant give and take, a tug-of-war, yin-and-yang-type balancing act, and in the end, the squeakiest wheel usually gets the most grease. Public perception and awareness combined with empathy or a tinge of moral indignation can frequently overcome societal indifference.

However, most of us aren't particularly altruistic when it comes to animals, and as such, aren't burdened by such weighty, enigmatic problems that border on the metaphysical. By extension, John Donne had it right when he wrote,

> If a clod be washed away from the sea, Europe is the less, as well as if a promontory were, as well as if a manor of thy friend's or of thine own were: any man's death diminishes me, because I am involved in mankind, and therefore never send to know for whom the bell tolls; it tolls for thee.

The same thing could and certainly is said about animals. Nevertheless, it's a moral weight many people are understandably unwilling or unable to shoulder.

In the real world, the one most of us live in most of the time, very few individuals have enough in their emotional checking account to really care in a viable, practical sense about the endangered saltwater Florida vole, the Atlantic salt marsh snake, the bluetail mole skink, the Enterprise spring snail, and other threatened or endangered species.

There are countless other animals—some furred, some feathered, some scaled—who are hanging on to their existence by a figurative eyelash. Eking out a living in complete obscurity, they often pass into oblivion/extinction with only a select number of people even being aware of their fate.

As a rule, we aren't particularly concerned with critters we can't see, wouldn't recognize even if we did, and probably never will see. Hectic, overburdened, techno-driven lives constantly make increasing demands on our time, emotions, and how we spend our waking hours, and the resulting and necessary prioritizing leaves little room to care in a proactive manner about many deserving creatures.

Animals appeal to us in different ways for different reasons, some of which are obvious, some not so apparent. Sea turtles have large, empathy-producing eyes; pandas invite cuddles; deer are equated with Bambi; Cape buffalo, one of the most dangerous animals in Africa, remind us of dim-witted, cud-chewing domesticated cows; and large felines such as lions or cheetahs are seen as nothing more than overgrown versions of household cats.

Strange as it may sound, crocodilians are "sexy" (to use media parlance) because people like to read about them. Even though they ride low in the water, they have a high public profile—sometimes for the right reasons; usually for the wrong.

Every now and then, one of them will take off somebody's arm or leg or eat the reckless adult, child, or unwary dog. Reporting of such events helps sell newspapers and makes for a macabre but attention-grabbing sixty-second sound byte on the local news. For the alligator or crocodile, it's definitely bad press, and whenever possible or practical, the offending animal is usually found and killed.

Generally speaking, people have a rarely understood and often subconscious fascination with animals that can and would (if given the chance) literally eat them. It's a paradoxical attraction, sometimes not without its own risks. We are the most highly evolved species on the planet, and as befits our position, are rightfully at the top of the food chain.

However, positions get reversed every now and then, either by accident or design, and we find ourselves taken down a notch or two. Instead of being top dog, we're suddenly the runt of the litter, and are forced to interact with animals who aren't particularly impressed with our collective achievements. To many of them we're just another potential meal, and a rather easy one at that.

Hunting and photographic safaris have always been a big business. African game parks are saturated with overcrowded minibuses filled to the gunwales with neck-craning, camera-laden tourists who pay a lot of money to observe and photograph large, exotic game animals, up close and personal. But our interest goes far beyond shooting animals, whether it be with a big-bore rifle, shotgun, bow and arrow, or telephoto lens.

Hippos kill more people in Africa than any other animal including lions, hyenas, and Cape buffalo. Turn on Animal Planet, the Discovery Channel, *National Geographic* specials, or any other nature-themed television program, and what do you see? Usually the big cats, such as lions, leopards, and cheetahs; truck-sized crocodiles; and highly venomous snakes. If given the choice, what would you rather watch: a fat hippo lazily munching on grass, or sports car–sleek lionesses taking down a Cape buffalo?

It's riveting to watch Steve Irwin (aka the Crocodile Hunter) grapple with man-eating crocs, or Rob Bredl (aka the Barefoot Bushman) pick up venomous snakes the way other people would handle blown-down twigs or tree limbs, or the photographer and self-proclaimed Snakemaster, Austin Stevens, getting those unbelievable close-ups of king cobras while dodging bullet-fast strikes. It gets and holds our attention. Even though these conservationists/biologists (like the equally telegenic Jeff Corwin) often talk about benign animals, they always manage to incorporate danger into their shows because they know it sells.

Many people like to be scared out of their wits as long as they feel they have some control over the situation. Skydivers, cliff jumpers, bungee jumpers, or amusement park thrill riders are examples of people who willingly participate in hair-raising activities.

Despite safety precautions, however, accidents do occasionally happen. Chutes fail to open, and we watch, horrified, as a hapless victim pinwheels out of control to the ground, landing with a sickening thud. Or a roller-coaster car derails and leaves screaming, petrified riders hanging precariously high above the ground. For the most part, these thrill seekers know (or have reasonable assurance) that when they strap on a chute or get into a roller coaster, it's going to be a round trip.

On the other hand, put yourself in proximity to a hungry lion, hyena, or Australian saltwater crocodile, and it's a whole different set of parameters. Hanging upside down on the Mind Blaster Super Ride at your favorite amusement park while the local fire department mills around and tries to figure out how to get you down is one thing. Getting tagged by a cobra or attacked by a lion or crocodile is quite another.

This has not gone unnoticed by Hollywood and major European film studios. Movies that feature alligators, crocodiles, or snakes have been produced with a fairly consistent frequency over the years. And for good reason.

The Internet Movie Database (www.imdb.com) lists twenty-one different theatrical movies with the word "alligator" in the title, beginning with *Pa Fishes in an Alligator Pond* (1916). In addition, the site lists sixteen films, one television movie, and one video game in which alligators figure prominently in the plot. No doubt there are more.

Crocodiles are represented by fifty-two theatrical movies principally produced in the United States, China, France, the Netherlands, Germany, and Russia, and one television movie. Other, smaller-market countries also make croc-themed flicks. Crocodiles figure in the plot of at least thirty-eight additional theatrical movies, including the rather intriguingly titled *Her Jungle Love* (1938).

Snakes are in the titles of twenty-one theatrical movies, three television movies, one television series, and six video games. They play significant roles in the plot of at least an additional 165 theatrical movies, including cameos in the Indiana Jones films and the fabulously titled *SSSSSSS* (1973). Represented countries include the United States, Brazil, India, China, Germany, and Italy.

Reptiles are big business.

Not all of these films are schlock quickies. Although many were made in a matter of weeks—with correspondingly wretched production values and B-list actors, and showings in second-tier theaters (or even straight-to-video release)—some were not.

While movies with crocodilians typically don't win awards, they have grossed millions worldwide. The Indiana Jones series featured snakes and alligators in minor but scene-stealing roles. In one James Bond film, *Live and Let Die* (1973), crocodiles were supposed to be used, but location filming in Florida required the use of alligators instead. Another example is the rather fantastical *Lake Placid* (1999), with Bridget Fonda and Bill Pullman, in which a giant, croclike reptile threatens the serenity of a small lake.

Other films were not as successful, but nevertheless fulfilled their mission: to give viewers a series of safe, cheap, somewhat predictable, relatively entertaining thrills. Hollywood clearly knows that it pays to make films about reptiles.

Pull out a harmless corn snake from a sack in a room full of people and many of them will jump out of their shoes trying to put distance between themselves and the snake. Show them a juvenile alligator or crocodile, and they'll instinctively recoil; there will be an increased pulse rate, a tightening of stomachs, and mild anxiety.

When the self-promoting Steve Irwin feeds his crocs, the audience loudly gasps in a combination of awe, fear, and revulsion at the sight of a minivan-sized saltie leaping out of the water and loudly snapping its jaws.

Why are people so afraid of alligators, crocodiles, and snakes? Is it because gators and crocs are ambush hunters—meaning, they're sneaky and don't fit into our definition of fair play? Other carnivorous animals also ambush their prey. Lionesses and every other big cat stalk and chase, seeking out the old, lame, or sick. There's nothing new where stalking is concerned. It's a tried-and-true system for getting a meal.

Is it because alligators and crocodiles (and caiman and gharials), with their beady-looking eyes, are not particularly attractive to most people? Or is it their large, pointy, and very conspicuous teeth regularly on display? Perhaps it's their habitat; alligators, crocodiles, caiman, and gharials live in freshwater swamps, rivers, and marshes, although a few prefer saltwater environments.

Is there a subliminal connection in people's minds between our modern-day swamps and the primeval ooze where all life began? Are we prejudiced against alligators and crocodiles because they often prefer to lurk below the surface in tea-colored water? And when they do show themselves on riverbanks or mounds, brazenly sunning with mouths agape, do we resent them because they seem to be flaunting their size and strength? Do they make us feel inferior in ways we do not understand?

Are people who are attracted to reptiles masochistic, or suicidal? Or a combination of both? Yes, to all of the above.

Because they have no arms or legs, snakes are obliged to crawl on the ground (although many of them are arboreal and aquatic). Their venom (unlike brandished teeth) is somewhat abstract because you can't see it, unless it's in a vial or dripping from the business end of a fang. It's usually a pale-yellow concoction of proteins, enzymes, and peptides (among other chemical compositions) that does very nasty things to humans and other animals.

By their very nature, fangs are repugnant. They are secretive weapons, hidden in the roof of the mouth, and also, extremely deadly: When they come out, they're extended too fast for the human eye to see them. No doubt many people associate fangs with hypodermic needles, which in fact they are. If given the choice between being bitten by a warm-blooded animal like a dog, or a cold-blooded animal like a snake (discounting venom), the majority of individuals would choose the former. Do we have a natural aversion to cold-blooded animals, and if so, why?

According to the University of Florida, alligators and crocodiles have killed on average one person a year for the past thirty years. If those odds aren't good enough for you, the National Safety Council says the chances of a person having contact with venomous snakes and lizards in any given year are 1 in 22,942,167, and 1 in 298,338 in the average lifetime. Your odds of being bitten or crushed by other reptiles in any given year are 1 in 8,880,839, and 1 in 115,486 in the average lifetime. The typical person has a better chance of winning a multimillion-dollar payoff in a state or national lottery.

The odds of being bitten or attacked by a dog are far greater, at 1 in 10,588,692 in a given year and 1 in 137,694 in the average lifetime. But if a survey was taken, more people would probably prefer an attack by a dog over a reptile or snake.

Ergo, warm-blooded animals are the chomp of choice.

CHAPTER TWO

APPETITES AND FUNCTIONS

PHYLUM: Chordata
SUBPHYLUM: Vertebrata
ORDER: Crocodilia
FAMILY: 1. **Crocodylidae**

American	*Crocodylus acutus*
Cuban	*C. rhombifer*
Johnston's	*C. johnstoni*
Mindoro	*C. mindorensis*
Morelet's	*C. moreletii*
Mugger	*C. palustris*
Nile	*C. niloticus*
New Guinea	*C. novaeguineae*
Orinoco	*C. intermedius*
Saltwater	*C. porosus*
Slender-snout	*C. cataphractus*
Siamese	*C. siamensis*
African Dwarf	*Osteolaemus tetraspis*
Congo Dwarf	*O. t. osborni*

PHYLUM: Chordata
SUBPHYLUM: Vertebrata
ORDER: Crocodilia

FAMILY:	2.	Alligatoridae	
		American	*Alligator mississippiensis*
		Chinese	*Alligator sinensis*
	3.	**Caiman**	
		Spectacled	*Caiman crocodilus*
		Brown	*Caiman c. fuscus*
		Jacaré	*C. c. yacare*
		Rio Apaporis	*C. c. apaporiensis*
		Broad-nosed	*C. latirostris*
		Black	*Melanosuchus niger*
		Cuvier's Dwarf	*Paleosuchus palpebrosus*
		Smooth-front (aka Schneider's Dwarf Caiman)	*P. trigonatus*
	4.	**Gavialidae**	
		False Gharial	*Tomistoma schlegelii*
		Gharial	*Gavialis gangeticus*

■ ■ Crocodilians and alligators are found between the latitudes of Cancer (23.5 degrees north) and Capricorn (23.5 degrees south) in the lakes, rivers, swamps, marshes, and canals of the southern United States, Cuba, Central and South America, Africa, Asia, and Australia. The average croc or gator will increase its size by approximately 4,000 from the time it is a hatchling to when it reaches adulthood.

All crocodilians, even the smaller species, are capable of eating people. However, many species live in remote areas where record keeping is unknown. Some crocs are reclusive and shy, while other species have very limited to virtually no contact with people. The American alligator (*Alligator mississippiensis*), Australian saltwater crocodile, Nile crocodile, and mugger crocodile account for the majority of fatal attacks on humans. (*Alligator* is derived from the Spanish *el lagarto*, which means "the lizard." *Mississippiensis* means "of the Mississippi," derived from *mississippi* plus *ensis*, which is Latin for "belonging to.")

Alligators are the unheralded undertakers of the swamps, marshes, lakes, ponds, and rivers they inhabit. Although adult alligators are at the top of their particular food chain, and are capable of killing (and more than willing to eat) anything they can catch, alligators will also happily feed on carrion if the opportunity arises, and they are hungry enough.

Alligators are opportunistic, ambush hunters. If it lives in the swamps, marshes, lakes, or rivers, sooner or later an alligator will catch it and eat it. Raccoons, skunks, birds of all types and sizes, muskrats, otters, turtles, fish, rats, skates, rays, salamanders, eels, juvenile alligators, snakes, and anything else it can get its jaws around are fair game for a hungry alligator.

Death plies its trade in alligator habitat, and carrion has definite advantages over live prey. For one thing, it doesn't fight back, eliminating the chance of possible injury to the alligator. Second, because the cellular breakdown has already been initiated, carrion is easier to digest. It also requires a lot less energy to obtain and absorb. Alligators have been known to stash a kill under logs or rocks underwater and let them "cure" for a couple of days before eating. Consumption of carrion also helps to prevent pollution.

Because they can digest bacteria-laden carrion with no ill effects, and live in stagnant waters without becoming sick, alligators make excellent subjects for immunological studies. Tests done at McNeese State University in Lake Charles, Louisiana, revealed that alligators have a serum compliment system that enables them to remain disease free while eating things that would probably kill a human. Whether these tests will have a practical use remains to be seen. In and of itself, the discovery of the serum compliment system adds another component to the alligator's remarkable adaptability.

Alligators (and some species of crocodiles) also help to cull the non-gamefish that in recent years have become endemic in some swamps, lakes, and rivers. These species often take over habitat occupied by native fishes and either kill all of them outright over a period of time, or severely reduce their numbers. Several types of perch, platyfish, pulchers, oscars, carp, catfish, and eels often successfully compete for resources native fishes depend on for their livelihood.

The state of Florida and all other states where alligators are found derive a great deal of money from recreational fishing. Licenses, tax revenues from a variety of sources, tourism, the sale of fishing gear, the sale of boats (and everything that goes with them)—all of this adds up to a considerable annual sum. When exotic species drive out native species, it not only adversely affects the natural balance of things, but can also have a deleterious effect on the state's coffers. Human removal of exotic, nonnative species is labor-intensive, time-consuming, and costly, and numerous county, state, and federal regulating agencies have strict guidelines that often make human intervention impractical, if not impossible.

While it is impossible to put an exact number on how many non-native or exotic fishes are taken by alligators annually, the sheer number of alligators makes the extrapolated number considerable.

Alligators are also dredgers and excavators. The yearly nests that the females laboriously and meticulously construct contribute to the environment in several ways. Fabricated from crushed nonaquatic and aquatic vegetation such as maidencane, bulrush and cattail, leaves, stalks, and other detritus, these nests are relatively large structures that can be 2 to 4 feet high, and 7 feet in diameter.

As they slowly waddle their way over their preferred terrain, these four-legged bulldozers, with their penchant for harvesting dross for nest building, have over millions of years added significantly to the above-water real estate in much of their habitat.

The preferred sites are elevated banks or high ground, although they will build on level ground if they have no choice. Typically the nests are situated (on average) between 3 and 20 feet from the nearest water. Using relatively stable and consistent yearly water levels as a reference in the same way as Nile crocodiles, the female calculates the nest location and height in an effort to ensure that her eggs are not threatened by sub-terranean flooding. Construction is sometimes abandoned for reasons not yet completely understood by scientists, and nests can be damaged or destroyed by unexpected rises in water levels or severe predation. Flooding and/or long periods of torrential rain (not unusual occurrences in alligator habitats) return rotted plant material from the nests to their source, enriching additional habitats.

Peat, a rotted, moisture-absorbing plant material, is often a by-product of alligator nests. If dried out properly, it can be burned for fuel (but obviously has to be harvested). In alligator habitat, it acts as a natural fire retardant, a welcome dynamic in dry season when wildfires (some of them quite large and potentially dangerous to humans) are the norm.

Though water is their preferred habitat, alligators are quite ambulatory, if in a lumbering way. They're obviously heavy animals, with short legs and belly low to the ground, and when they go from one place to the other, they leave trails behind—places where they've flattened out the ground. These trails are an important factor in the flow of water through the Everglades—and all other alligator habitats—and also to the formation of buttonwood strands.

As they slowly waddle along, they tear the roots of mangroves and other vegetation with their snouts and tails. In doing so, they keep the mangrove creeks open. However, when alligator populations decline, mangrove roots grow and accumulate debris. Over time mangrove creeks are taken over by buttonwood trees and become strands.

The nests are also a source of food for raccoons and other animals either brazen or hungry and quick enough to steal the eggs that are a somewhat abundant, excellent source of protein.

After they are abandoned, alligator nests provide excellent habitat for many species of small mammals who burrow into them, forming tunnels, living quarters, food storage rooms, and birth chambers. Not only do these nests provide already-constructed housing for these mammals, but often, they are sturdier and better homes than the new occupiers could have built themselves. Additionally, because they are relatively large, alligator nests can support greater numbers of mammals than individual dens or tunnels, in what is essentially communal living.

There is also another benefit. As they thrive, these small mammals breed and enter the food chain, which is, of course, dominated by the alligator. Many species that occupy alligator nests do in fact wind up being eaten by the former occupants, thus completing and propagating the circle of life and death that characterizes the habitat.

During the dry season when the alligator "landlords" vacate their nest premises, birds and terrestrial animals move in, seeking needed and welcome refuge in the cool, temperature-regulated mounds. Many of these animals also seek refuge in the mounds during the wet season when monsoonlike rains flood their own dens and threaten them with death by drowning.

Alligator holes—a series of tunnels and craters created to conserve water during the dry season—are also refuges for fishes, frogs, crabs, and turtles, many of whom pay the ultimate in rent to their reptile landlords when they wind up as a meal. These holes are often the only source of water for miles, attracting birds who nest in the trees above them. Landlord alligators wait patiently below for an easy feed in the form of chicks who fall from the safety of their nests.

Because the water is so deep, the holes attract gamefish that in turn attracts fishermen. However, the primary functions of the holes are to provide alligators with a cool spot in summer, a warm place in winter, and a nursery for hatchlings.

Alligators also have another intrinsic value. Obviously, they play a vital role in maintaining their habitat, as do other animals; but no matter how large they get or how ferocious they may look, they are but one denizen of an environment that includes many different animals who have equally important roles to play. On an innate level, all animals have an equal value, and it makes no difference if they are scaled, feathered, or furred, small or large, pretty or ugly, nocturnal or diurnal, venomous or nonvenomous. Ethically and morally, they are all equally deserving of compassion and protection under the law.

The different state and federal regulating agencies do not discriminate, they classify: endangered, threatened, a species of special concern, native and nonnative, or exotic. To a great extent, justice is blind, and the governing bodies are required by law to act in ways that reflect that credo. They cannot nor should they be required to play God.

The individuals who work for the agencies are often under tremendous pressure from both within and without. Frequently understaffed, they do an admirable job in protecting and managing all animals irrespective of their personal favorites.

Their employers, such as the National Park Service, are subject to extraordinary political coercion from a variety of sources, some of which wield considerable clout. Washington, D.C., is home to thousands of lobbyists representing a variety of often-conflicting interests. Governmental administrations from the federal level on down all have agendas that frequently put them in direct conflict with the animals. These conflicts can and do result in the elimination or reduction of both habitat and species numbers, and extinctions are not unknown.

CHAPTER THREE

CONTACT WITH PEOPLE— NOT A GOOD IDEA

■ ■ Although confined for the most part to the southeastern quadrant of the United States, the habitat of *Alligator mississippiensis* is nevertheless geographically far-reaching and varied, and includes lakes, rivers, streams, marshes, canals, and swamps. The northern reaches of its territory are the coastal region of North Carolina, while the southern extremity includes the vast expanses of Florida's Everglades and adjacent Big Cypress Swamp. American alligators can also be found in South Carolina's Savannah River and its tributaries and many swamps; in the southern half of Georgia, including the Okefenokee Swamp that overlaps into northern Florida; and in Alabama's Mobile Delta region.

Alligators have moved westward as well, making themselves at home in central and southern Mississippi, all the bayous and swamps found throughout Louisiana, parts of Arkansas, the eastern third of Texas, and Oklahoma's Red River and Little River drainages in the southeastern part of the state.

The mating season is prime conflict time between humans and alligators. Large males in search of mates will freely move between bodies of water, and in doing so cross roadways and frequently trespass on private property, often placing them in uncomfortable proximity to humans. The Florida Fish and Wildlife Conservation Commission (FWC) removes around 4,000 alligators per year in an effort to reduce the potential for conflicts. Other states eliminate a proportional number of alligators.

Nuisance alligators are made, not born. Florida receives nearly 1,000 new residents a day, many of them retirees from colder northern states or regions where alligators do not live. Ignorant of alligators' habits and regarding them as a novelty or harmless curiosity, newly arrived people often feed them, which is both illegal in Florida (punishable by sixty days in jail and a $500 fine) and extremely dangerous. In Texas, intentionally feeding a free-ranging alligator is a Class C misdemeanor punishable by a fine of up to $500.

The increase in human population (and our insatiable desire for waterfront living) combined with a 5 percent boost in the alligator population creates an exponentially factored rise in the probability of human-alligator encounters. Although they are naturally shy and have an innate fear of humans, once an alligator loses its fear and starts to associate people with food, it can become quite threatening. Then, it can be classified as a nuisance alligator, subjecting it to removal and death. People routinely exercise amazingly poor judgment, having their pictures taken while standing perilously close to an alligator, and sometimes placing themselves between an alligator and water, blocking the animal's escape route and leaving it with little or no choice.

Large sums of money are spent annually in public education programs at the state, county, and local levels, reaching out to everyone from preteens to senior citizens in an effort to try to convince them that alligators and people *can* coexist. The FWC has made two brochures available to the public: "Living with Alligators" and "American Alligator." Conspicuous signs are posted by rivers, lakes, and canals that are known to contain alligators.

Despite their inherent danger, these creatures are also an important part of Florida's wetlands, and besides their ecological value, they attract many tourists. Approximately half a million people visit the Everglades National Park every year, and the significant amount of money they spend does not go unnoticed by public officials.

Although alligators can tolerate a reasonable degree of salinity for short periods of time, and are occasionally found in brackish water around mangrove swamps, they lack the buccal salt-secreting glands that are found in crocodiles. Because of that, they are pretty much restricted to freshwater. It doesn't have to be particularly clean, just fresh. A nice, murky swamp will do just fine.

To the eye untrained in the science of dendrology (the study of trees), all lakes tend to look alike. A body of freshwater in upstate New York will appear to be very similar, at least to the average eye, to a lake in South Carolina, Florida, or Texas. Moreover, lakes conjure up images of boating, fishing, and swimming under a hot summer sun, and these stunning pictures of clear water and verdant trees are often redolent of fast-fading childhood memories.

A swamp is quite another matter.

For one thing, they're spooky. The water is typically dark, and there's no telling what's in it. Anything could be lurking just beneath the surface, and it's probably best not to stick your big toe in to test the water's temperature. Light filters down from the overhead canopy creating a disorienting, chiaroscuro pattern. A seemingly haphazard placement of trees and hammocks defies logic and makes navigation by boat or canoe difficult. Unseen animals suddenly splash loudly and alarmingly in the water as the visitor slowly navigates through the labyrinth. You get the feeling you're being watched. People with overactive imaginations begin to feel very uncomfortable. Land is confined to isolated, often small islands, and it is very difficult to accurately ascertain the water's depth.

The Okefenokee National Wildlife Refuge is a 396,000-acre (approximately 700 square miles) bog inside a huge, saucer-shaped impression that was once part of the ocean floor. *Okefenokee* means "Land of the Trembling Earth" in the Seminole language. The swamp is between 103 to 128 feet above mean sea level, and the tea-colored waters are caused by tannic acid released from decaying vegetation. The swamp is 36 miles from north to south and roughly 25 miles from east to west. Prairies cover about 60,000 acres of the swamp and are home to numerous birds, including herons, egrets, ibises, cranes, and bitterns. There are over 400 vertebrate species; more than half are birds.

Representatives of fourteen families of fishes swim in the waterways, pools, and shrub and cypress swamps, including catfish, sunfish, bowfin, redfin, and pickerel. More than sixty species of reptiles live in the swamp, including thirty-six species of snakes, five of which are venomous. Lizards are represented by eleven species, turtles by fourteen, and native mammals by thirty different species, including raccoon, skunk, and white-tailed deer.

It is also prime alligator habitat.

A study performed for the National Wetlands Research Center found that alligators ingest a wide variety of food items. Variation in their diet was attributed to the type of habitat occupied, prey species encountered, prey vulnerability and size, and the size of the alligators themselves. The findings corresponded to an earlier study which found that for alligators living in three lakes in north-central Florida, fish species were the most important food item. Invertebrates had a low percentage volume. Reptiles ranked second in percentage volume. Turtles were the most common reptile, and the most important food for alligators that exceeded 3 meters in length. Young alligators ate more invertebrates and terrestrial prey than did larger alligators. Adult females also consumed more mammals than did adult males. Alligators in Florida as a rule tend to consume more fish and turtles and fewer mammals than alligators in other parts of this species' range.

Another study of adult alligator diets in various types of marshes in southwestern Louisiana found that vertebrates (mammals, birds, reptiles, and fish) were the most important class of foods taken.

During 1961–62 and 1964, hunters on the Sabine National Wildlife Refuge in southwest Louisiana (where water salinities range from near-fresh to brackish) killed 413 alligators. When researchers examined their stomach contents, they found that crustaceans and fish were important foods for alligators that were longer than approximately five feet long.

Alligators are practical pragmatists who take advantage of whatever food sources are available to them. Because their food sources breed in substantial numbers, alligators do not impact one species to the detriment of another.

Which may explain why people are on the menu.

DEATH ON SANIBEL

Since 1948 there have been over 300 documented attacks on people by alligators in Florida. Only a small percentage have resulted in fatalities; however, some unfortunate, unlucky, or imprudent individuals constitute a grisly short list.

On July 21, 2004, fifty-four-year-old landscaper Janie Melsek was trimming vegetation beside a pond at a vacation rental property in a residential section of upscale Sanibel Island (Lee County), Florida. There are many ponds on Sanibel, and the tropical climate lends itself to consistent and rapid lush growth that must be pruned at regular intervals. About 6,100 people live on the island, which is located on the southwest coast near Fort Myers. The median age of residents is sixty, and the median house value is $392,400.

Vibrant and happy in her work, the petite victim had no idea she was being silently stalked by an 11-foot, 9-inch alligator as she contentedly snipped and pruned. Suddenly, the reptile darted out of the water and grabbed Melsek by her right arm. (The attack came from behind, indicating the victim might have been bending over at the time.) Melsek's neighbor Jim Anholt came running from across the

street, and with the help of three Sanibel police officers, he struggled for five desperate minutes to pull Melsek out of the water. Finally, the reptile reluctantly released her.

The animal disappeared, then resurfaced 20 feet away, opened
its mouth, and started swimming toward Melsek and the rescue
party. Police officers shot the alligator in the head, killing it instantly.
Six strong men were needed to lift and drag the 457-pound reptile
up on the shore.

In addition to her arm, which was amputated midway between
her elbow and wrist during six hours of surgery, the victim also received severe injuries to her buttocks and inner thighs. While doctors at Lee Memorial Hospital in Fort Myers initially believed she
would recover and eventually walk again, she died two days later on
July 23 as a result of infections caused by the bites.

People are under the misconception that as long as they aren't
fed, even large alligators will shy away from people.

"That's an old wives' tale," said alligator expert Lindsey Hord of
the Florida Fish and Wildlife Conservation Commission. "Alligators
are predators, and under the right circumstances, can see a human
as a prey item.

"A nine-footer might be stretching the imagination thinking it
could take a human; it might be a case of mistaken identity, where it
grabs something swimming and says, 'Oh, this isn't a raccoon.' But
for a 10-footer, a 150-pound person is something it would be able
to take like a deer or hog. The majority of fatalities by big alligators
have been feeding attacks, seeing the person as a prey item."

Although a necropsy of the alligator that attacked Melsek
showed it had not been fed, authorities said they would not have
expected to find food remains in the alligator because of the animal's exceedingly strong digestive system.

In late April 2004, another Sanibel resident, Jane C. Keefer, seventy-
four, was attacked by a 9-foot, 7-inch-long alligator as she gardened

near a canal bank behind her home. It was around 8:00 P.M., and another beautiful summer sunset was about to unfold. Soon the island sky would be streaked with brilliant swaths of crimson, pink, and yellow. Waterfront bars and restaurants quickly filled with happy people enjoying the sun's spectacular descent into the blue-gray waters of the Gulf of Mexico.

While they were enjoying the view, Keefer found herself in a desperate life-and-death struggle as the reptile attempted to drag her into the water. With the help of her husband, who upon hearing her frantic cries for help had rushed to her aid, she struggled to remain on shore. Together they were able to fight the animal off. Keefer's injuries were successfully treated at HealthPark Medical Center, and she made a full recovery.

Subsequent to the fatal attack on Melsek, trappers killed at least 81 alligators on Sanibel Island. Experts estimate the alligator population on 12-mile-long Sanibel at approximately 300.

Lee County harvested 429 alligators in 2005, and 7,991 were harvested statewide as of December 2005, said Linda Collins, a spokeswoman for Florida's Statewide Nuisance Alligator Program.

DEATH BY ALLIGATOR

Sixteen-year-old Sharon Holmes has the dubious distinction of being the first individual on the list of people killed by alligators in Florida, since they started keeping track. On August 16, 1973, she was swimming at dusk in Oscar Scherer State Park in Sarasota County.

I have been to this park, and it's a lovely place. There's a small pond, and a fairly shallow and wide stream meanders through the grounds. Canoeing and tubing are popular recreational activities. Lurking alligators are usually the last thing people think about.

August is a very hot and humid month in Florida, and the cool waters must have been irresistible to Sharon. A necropsy on the 11-foot,

3-inch male alligator that killed her indicated it had been fed by park visitors.

On September 28, 1977, George Leonard, fifty-two, decided to take a swim in the Peace River in Charlotte County around 8:30 P.M. People often swim in the many rivers that crisscross Florida. However, this time the swimmer had company. A 7-foot female alligator suddenly appeared out of nowhere and fatally wounded him. He was not eaten, and experts concluded that the attack might have been a case of mistaken identity.

Phillip Rastrelli, fourteen, decided to swim across the Hidden River Canal in Martin County on September 10, 1978. He never made it to the other side. He was intercepted at 12:00 P.M. by an 11-foot male alligator that killed him. The victim was an opportune target for the gator.

A 12-foot, 4-inch male alligator in poor health decided that eleven-year-old Robert Crespo would make an easy-to-catch supper as the youngster was swimming in a canal in St. Lucie County at 4:30 P.M. on August 6, 1984. Crespo was eaten alive.

Children are easier to kill than adults. They have smaller limbs that can easily be torn off and swallowed whole by alligators. Unlike adults, they are less likely to fight back, and even if they do, resistance is usually short-lived and futile.

George Cummings III, a Florida State University student, was snorkeling in the Wakulla Springs State Park south of Tallahassee on July 13, 1987. The spring is North America's largest and deepest, the water cold and clear, and it's popular with both tourists and locals. George foolishly left the well-posted, restricted swimming area and started to lazily float down the Wakulla River. He should have known better—and he paid the ultimate price for his mistake.

Instead of bass and bream, he found himself face-to-face with an 11-foot male alligator that effortlessly killed him at about 2:00 P.M. A little while later, as a glass-bottomed boat cruised down the river, a tourist excitedly pointed out the alligator with a dead deer in its jaws—only the deer was George Cummings.

Erin Glover, four, was walking along the Hidden Lake shore in Charlotte County on June 4, 1988, perilously close to the water. A 10-foot, 7-inch male alligator ambushed her and ate her at 6:00 P.M. It was subsequently discovered that for months, neighbors had been buying groceries, mostly marshmallows, to feed the alligator. Unfortunately, as is so often the case, an innocent victim paid for the mistakes and ignorance of others.

Three-year-old Adam Binford made the fatal mistake of straying outside a roped-off swimming area at Lake Ashby in Volusia County on March 21, 1997. Children are naturally curious and often wander where they shouldn't. His lifeless, horribly mutilated body was recovered the next day about a mile from the attack site. An 11-foot alligator suspected of the attack was later killed by a trapper.

Samuel Wetmore's life came to an unexpected end on May 4, 2001, when he took a dip in a pond near his home in Venice in Sarasota County. Wetmore was seventy years old and no doubt near the end of his life expectancy. Nevertheless, there are far better ways to meet one's maker. His floating body was found with an 8-foot alligator still cautiously circling it. The victim died of trauma and blood loss.

On June 23, 2001, two-year-old Alexandria Murphy was dragged into Lake Cannon in Polk County. Unobserved, she had wandered away from her fenced backyard in Winter Haven and was killed by a 6-foot, 6-inch alligator, just 700 feet from her home.

The gator had drowned the helpless child, but both arms and a leg were punctured by bites, and the child's delicate bones were broken in several places. A trapper easily caught the animal, which was accustomed to people—probably because it had been fed. A gruesome discovery was made when the gator's jaws were examined, and human hair was found inside.

On September 11, 2001, Robert Steele, eighty-two, was walking his dog on a narrow trail between two wetland areas in the J. N. "Ding" Darling National Wildlife Refuge on Sanibel Island. The Refuge is a popular place for observing a variety of wildlife. In this particular case, the wildlife had been observing Steele. He was attacked and killed while he walked the peaceful trail. Later, Florida Wildlife Commission officers killed a 10-foot, 6-inch gator suspected of the attack.

On June 18, 2003, in Lake County, twelve-year-old Brian Griffin was suddenly attacked while swimming near a boat ramp in the ominously named Dead River at about 8:00 P.M. The alligator was 10 feet, 4 inches long, weighed 339 pounds, and was subsequently destroyed along with several other large gators. It pulled the youth underwater for at least twenty-five minutes. The gator surfaced once with the boy in its jaws, shocking and horrifying helpless witnesses who could do nothing to save the boy.

In Lee County several months after Janie Melsek was killed, twenty-year-old Georgia resident Michelle Reeves inexplicably went swimming after midnight in a retention pond at Lee Memorial Health Park. Apparently nobody bothered telling her that it was more than likely alligators were in the pond. Swimming in ponds or any other body of water is never a good idea in Florida, especially at night when unseen alligators are likely to be on the prowl.

Reeves was found floating facedown with her right arm bitten off at the elbow and deep puncture marks on her body. A 7-foot, 11-inch alligator later captured by wildlife officers was found to have human body parts in its stomach. An autopsy determined Reeves had drowned due to the attack. Reeves was an English major at Georgia State University in Atlanta.

In Lakeland on March 15, 2005, fishermen in Six Pound Pond discovered the body of fifty-six-year-old Don Owen, a truck driver from Bartow (about twelve miles away). He had been missing since March 9. Trappers later caught an 8-foot, 9-inch, 300-pound alligator that had Owen's forearm in its stomach. It was later determined that the alligator had been fed by area residents.

Kevin Albert Murray, forty-one, of North Port, Florida, worked hard at his lawn maintenance job, so it was only natural that on a Friday evening in July 2005, he decided to cool off by going for a swim in a canal in the Apollo Waterway.

The imprudent Murray swam into eternity. The vehicle for his demise was a 12-foot, 2-inch-long alligator that wasted no time in grabbing him by an arm and pulling him under the water.

Murray was in good physical condition. As he was being dragged under the water, he kicked and thrashed around wildly, hitting the alligator as hard as he could with his free hand. Witnesses reported that he struggled to reach the surface, which he briefly did. Determined not to lose its meal, the alligator renewed its attack, and was finally able to drag the victim under the water and drown him. It happened so quickly that the stunned witnesses were unable to save Murray's life.

The week beginning on Monday, May 8, 2006, will go down in history as one of the deadliest in terms of fatal attacks by alligators in Florida. Within a span of six horrific days, gators claimed three victims—all female, and all young.

■ ■ ■

Yovy Suarez Jimenez, a twenty-eight-year-old law student, was the first to die in what was to be a time of unprecedented carnage wreaked on the citizens of the Sunshine State by an unforgiving predator.

On Tuesday, the petite blonde went for a jog at approximately 7:00 P.M. along a bicycle path that ran parallel to a canal in the south Florida city of Sunrise, a suburb northwest of Fort Lauderdale. She was last heard from at roughly 9:30 P.M. when her mother called her on her cell phone. The victim said she was sitting under a bridge near a canal, feeling depressed. Yovy lived in a mobile home park a few miles away, and was a student at Florida Atlantic University.

Officer Jorge Pino, a spokesman for the Florida Fish and Wildlife Conservation Commission, said witnesses had seen a woman matching Jimenez's description, dangling her feet over the water's edge. The victim was wearing Nike trainers running shoes, cycling shorts, and a sports bra. No one saw the actual attack.

The following day, construction workers found the victim's badly mutilated body floating in the canal between Markham Park and State Road 84. Apparently the killer gator had stalked Jimenez and dragged her into the water.

"We have physical evidence to support our theory that the young lady was dragged into the water and attacked," said Pino. "But that's a theory. We may never know. The possibility also exists that she might have fallen in."

"The alligator attacked her and basically amputated her arms, bit her on the right leg and back, and pulled her into the water," said Dr. Joshua Perper, the Broward County medical examiner who performed the autopsy. "She died extremely fast. By the time she was pulled into the water, she was already dead." Dr. Perper also said the victim had been very close to the water's edge when the gator attacked her, because her body showed no signs of being dragged.

The victim's arms had been severed near her shoulders. The official cause of death was traumatic injuries sustained by an alligator attack, a combination of shock and blood loss. Drowning was eliminated as a cause of death because little water was found in the victim's lungs and stomach.

The attack was the first fatal gator attack ever recorded in Broward County. The assault was also unusual because it occurred on land. Typically, gators (and all crocodilians) launch attacks from the water, although they will travel on land in order to get a meal.

Did the gator stalk the victim, as was suggested by several newspaper accounts? It is possible the gator could have followed the victim, who perhaps stopped and allowed the gator to close the distance between them.

Another feasible scenario is that the alligator was simply lying perfectly concealed in tall grasses next to the jogging path. It was night, the sun had long since disappeared into the horizon, and it would have been almost impossible to see the alligator because its black-colored hide would have rendered it nearly invisible.

Resting in the grass, the opportunistic gator saw a tasty meal coming toward it, and when the moment was right, leapt up and out, grabbing the victim by a leg and pulling her to the ground, where it proceeded to amputate her arms with the subtlety and effectiveness of a meat cleaver.

After the victim was dead, the gator then dragged her lifeless body into the safety of the water. Several days later, licensed hunters caught a 9-foot, 6-inch-long gator. In its stomach were the partially digested arms.

Four days later, and several hours' drive to the west in the central part of Florida, twenty-three-year-old Annemarie Campbell, a resident of Paris, Tennessee, was snorkeling in a lake in a secluded recreation area approximately 50 miles southeast of Gainesville, and

7 miles south of Salt Springs. The lake is near Lake George, which in turn is close to the Ocala National Forest in Marion County. Campbell had been staying at an isolated cabin near a springhead that feeds into the lake.

Was Ms. Campbell aware of the fate that had recently befallen Ms. Jimenez? If she was, would it have made any difference? The victim was obviously preoccupied with observing the underwater life as she blissfully floated on the water's surface, and was unaware that another, much larger and infinitely more dangerous denizen of the lake was observing her with intense interest.

A large alligator appeared out of nowhere, like a living nightmare, and clamped its massive jaws around her, exerting over 2,000 pounds of jaw pressure on the victim's body. Death must have been almost instantaneous.

Marion County fire-rescue Captain Joe Amigliori said the people she was staying with came out of the cabin, and to their horror, found her inside the gator's mouth. Exhibiting a complete disregard for their own safety, they jumped into the water and somehow managed to pull the victim out of the gator's mouth.

Annemarie Campbell was pronounced dead at the scene. The victim's stepfather, who took part in the futile attempt to save Annemarie, was treated at the scene for minor injuries, including lacerations and bite wounds to his hand.

On the same day, May 14, the body of forty-three-year-old Judy W. Cooper of Dunedin was discovered floating in a canal in an Oldsmar subdivision, 20 miles north of St. Petersburg in Pinellas County, which is around 120 miles southwest of Ocala. According to the local medical examiner's office, her upper body had bite marks consistent with an alligator attack. The victim, whose body had been in the water for approximately three days, completed the terrible trifecta of fatal alligator attacks.

CLOSE ENCOUNTERS

Not all attacks are fatal, nor do they all involve humans.

On May 24, 2004, Rick Cabot, pastor of the First United Methodist Church, was attacked by a 6-foot, 9-inch alligator in Lutz, Florida. In a proven killing technique, the gator pulled Cabot under the water. The pastor had the sense, or the nerve (or the desperation) to punch the gator in its nose. This caused the reptile—who clearly intended to inflict great bodily harm—to release Cabot. Fortunately, the pastor made a full recovery.

Twelve-year-old Malcolm Locke was swimming in Lake Diana just north of Orlando on May 20, 2004, when a 3- to 4-foot-long alligator bit him on his head and dragged him under the water. The boy courageously fought the gator, which released him. The alligator was subsequently removed by trappers.

Overly curious dogs who go into the water or venture too close to lakes, canals, and rivers where alligators live are regarded as just another prey item.

Jimmy Jordan was walking his golden retriever, Pete, along a lakeshore in St. Petersburg in late April 1999. He whistled for the unleashed dog, and then watched, frozen in horror, as a nightmare unfolded.

"As soon as Pete looked back at me, the alligator grabbed him by his whole head and whipped him into the water, and was gone. This could easily have been a child. This thing could have taken anybody, anything just as quickly as it took an 86-pound dog," said Jordan.

Even people who should know better are not immune from attacks. In September 2002, Dan Goodman, fifty-four, director of the Kanapaha Botanical Gardens near Gainesville, Florida, was weeding in a

3-foot-deep lily pond when he inadvertently stepped on a submerged and obviously well-camouflaged 10-foot-long male alligator. The gator instantly lunged up and clamped his powerful jaws on Goodman's right arm, severing it just below the elbow and swallowing it.

Wildlife officials said the 388-pound reptile lived in a nearby pond and occasionally ventured into the lily pond, where it had become used to people.

Goodman's splashing was mistaken for prey, causing an immediate attack response. The reptile was killed and the severed arm removed from the gator's stomach, but it was too badly damaged to be reattached. Goodman survived the attack.

Most people associate the Kennedy Space Center in Cape Canaveral with astronauts and space shuttles. Cryogenics engineer Martin Hayes had a very unnerving experience there recently.

"I remember I was leaving work a little later than usual. Since I work at the Launch Pad (LC-39B), I have to go through the badge gate before I leave. Well, when I drove up to the badge gate, I was quite surprised. I got the opportunity to see a live alligator wrestling match. Apparently some of the local wildlife had wandered up to the badge board. Someone, of course, called the Fish and Wildlife guys. So there's this big, strong wildlife guy and an alligator about as long as his leg.

"The wildlife guy stands in front of the alligator—whose mouth is open, and he's hissing—and the guy dangles a rope with a noose at the end of it in front of him. He then tightens the noose around the gator's snout and pulls the gator forward. The alligator did not go quietly. The man and the gator played tug-of-war for quite some time. Finally the guy was able to get behind the gator, close his mouth, and wrap a rope around it. I finally went home—but that was some show."

Even small alligators can be dangerous. On October 6, 2005, twenty-five-year-old Danielle Rivera of Palm Bay, Florida, foolishly decided to feed a 3-foot-long alligator at Crane's Creek in downtown Melbourne. The gator leapt out of the water and bit her on the hand.

Rivera said she did not realize that alligators could propel themselves out of the water. Police officers issued Rivera a written warning for violating the state law that prohibits feeding wild alligators; trappers captured the gator, which was subsequently harvested.

An 11-foot, 385-pound alligator attacked Guy Daelemans, forty-three, as he was pulling weeds along the shallow shore of Lake Eustis in Lake County in central Florida. Daelemans saved himself by punching the reptile in the nose. Wildlife officials caught the alligator and destroyed it. There are no known repellents, toxicants, or fumigants for alligators. Weeding by lakeshores can often be hazardous to one's health.

Hurricane Katrina provided a grisly bonanza for the many alligators that happily inhabited New Orleans's adjacent swamps and marshlands. As Hank Finney paddled his small boat from house to house in his flooded neighborhood, trying to rescue people, he interrupted alligators who were feeding on the many dead, decomposing bodies that floated in the water. It must have been a horrible sight. Alligators are voracious eaters. They tear off hunks of flesh and swallow them whole.

"I was fighting off alligators, 4-foot alligators, beating them off. They were tearing up a dead body and I was just trying to beat them off. When I fell off [the boat], I scuffed myself trying to get back in the boat because they were coming after me," he said.

Finney had a narrow escape and was bitten several times in the process. The resulting infections from the bites were treated with antibiotics and he was expected to make a full recovery.

In all likelihood, alligators consumed many bodies after the hurricane. Untold numbers of people simply disappeared down the gullets of hungry gators who knew a good thing when they saw it.

Opportunity knocked and the gators answered. They also performed a macabre public service as natural undertakers.

In February 2006, the California Highway Patrol said it plans to fire two officers after an internal inquiry determined they used their service weapons to kill alligators after the hurricane. The unnamed officers were attached to a unit of Louisiana State Police troopers when they fired at gators in a bayou in the vicinity of New Orleans.

Officers are required by California Highway Patrol policy to report when they discharge their weapons, which these officers failed to do. They also broke Louisiana law when they killed at least one alligator.

Members of the Port Orange, Florida, police department speculated that when David Havenner, forty-one, attacked his girlfriend in their mobile home in July 2004 with a 3-foot-long alligator (which he'd kept in the bathtub), it was the first case on record of a gator being used as a weapon during a domestic dispute. Havenner was charged with misdemeanor battery and illegal possession of an alligator.

FLORIDA'S NUISANCE ALLIGATOR CONTROL PROGRAM

The Florida Fish and Wildlife Conservation Commission Alligator Management Program (aka, the nuisance alligator control program) was founded in 1978, and is administered by the Division of Law Enforcement. The program only destroys alligators that are four feet and longer, a size it regards as big enough to either kill a human or inflict serious injury. Those less than 4 feet are relocated. But this does not mean that an alligator smaller than 4 feet is not dangerous to humans. They can and will administer serious bites.

The state decided that any alligator that was to be killed had to have a commercial value associated with it. The state contracts forty authorized alligator trappers who are compensated solely from the selling of the hides and meat. The hides are sold to the state, and hunters receive 70 percent of the money associated with this sale. The remaining 30 percent is put toward the administrative costs of the program.

Moreover, research methods have been put in place to ascertain the maximum harvesting allowable while precluding population decreases. It was noted that alligators are demographically different from other game choices in Florida. For example, a single overharvest of deer will not impact population levels for a few years, but deleterious effects associated with overharvesting of crocodilians during a single season can be detected for quite some time.

Also recognized was the fact that while Louisiana has an excellent management program, Florida's is different due to the unique set of variables that exist. Harvesters in Louisiana fish for the males and non-reproductive females by searching certain canals. In Louisiana, the habitat of reproductive females does not overlap very much with the former groups. In Florida, however, this dichotomy of habitats does not exist, thereby preventing this type of management approach. The most effective approach has been to locate nests and remove the eggs while being aware of the impact that particular nest removal will have on the population.

Loss of habitat is arguably the main reason for alligator confrontations with man. What used to be basking or nesting areas ten years ago have been transformed into golf courses, swimming pools, and people's backyards. This should come as no surprise to anyone.

However, due in part to the nuisance alligator control program and increased public awareness, the number of alligator attacks that occur annually has remained constant in spite of the increases in alligator and human populations in Florida. During the last ten years, an average of only 3.6 severe attacks (fatalities or bites resulting in wounds requiring moderate to major medical care) occurred per year. Florida has more than 1.5 million residents and over 40 million user-occasions of humans in freshwater, such as swimming, wading, and so forth.

In 2001 there were 16,749 complaints of alligators threatening people, pets, or property, a record since the FWC began keeping a tally in

1997. More than 7,200 alligators judged to be a risk by game wardens were captured and killed.

Live capture is not as effective as killing when removing alligators. In the past, captured alligators were typically moved to more remote areas where it was hoped they would not cause further problems. However, this caused other potential problems; by placing tame or potentially aggressive alligators in areas where sportsmen and recreationers would not be expecting to find them, the risk of additional attacks was increased. In many cases, existing populations in wild areas were nearing their carrying capacity, and the addition of new, large alligators caused the displacement of existing alligators.

Since 1998 the FWC had identified open-permit areas where chronic dangerous situations occur, such as high-use water recreation areas, fish camps, boat ramps, public parks, and refuges. Approximately 33 percent of complaints result in the taking of an alligator. Nuisance alligator trappers are expected to operate discreetly and to present a favorable image to the public; in other words, make the kills clean, quick, and out of sight, if possible.

Less than half the recorded complaints resulted in alligator deaths. What about the rest—the remaining 9,549 complaints that were not deemed to be grave threats to humans?

Alligator complaints can usually be evaluated by a trained telephone operator and a decision can be quickly rendered based on the validity of the complaint. It is reasonable to assume that they involve smaller alligators, under the four-foot limit, which, while certainly irritating and perhaps a little anxiety-producing, posed no tangible threat to either property or human life. Compared to the total alligator population, the number of alligators destroyed annually is a tiny blip on the radar screen.

The majority of problems with alligators result when they wind up in places they are not wanted, like backyards, carports, and swimming pools. The number of nuisance alligators continues to rise annually because relocation habitats are dwindling. There's simply nowhere to put them, and as a result, they have to be sacrificed.

Compared with other animal attacks, the chances of encountering an alligator in ways you don't even want to think about are relatively slim. That's obviously no consolation to those unfortunate or imprudent individuals who have had frightening confrontations, but people face odds just about every time they engage in any activity, whether it's flying on an airplane, driving to the supermarket, or even taking a shower.

Other wild animals are known for their attacks against man.

Colorado had two fatal cougar (aka puma, mountain lion) attacks, both in the 1990s. Washington State had ten nonfatal attacks, eight of which occurred since 1990. Arizona reported three attacks in 2000. In 2001 a skier near Banff, Alberta, was mauled and bitten to death by a cougar, the first fatality in the province. A bicyclist on Vancouver Island, British Columbia, was attacked in the same year, but miraculously survived.

Black and grizzly bears accounted for 128 deaths in North America during the twentieth century. Fifty-six deaths occurred between 1980 and 2000. Between 1990 and 2000, black bears killed two people, and grizzlies terminated eighteen, even though the grizzly bear population is far less than that of the black bear. In the 1930s there was one fatal bear attack, and in the 1940s, there were six lethal assaults. In 2001 there were two fatal bear attacks, one in northern New Mexico and the other near Yellowknife in Canada.

Urban sprawl is certainly not unique to Florida, or any other state where alligators live. Home construction, its related public- and private-sector support industries, the jobs they create, and the much-needed tax revenues they generate (which fill county and state coffers) are very big business. The equation is simple: More people equals less suitable habitat equals an increase in attacks.

The Texas Parks and Wildlife Department (TPWD) estimates the alligator population of Jefferson, Liberty, and Orange counties to be 286,000. The total Texas population is approximately half a million alligators. In 1999 the Texas counties of Harris, Chambers, Liberty, Fort Bend, and Brazoria recorded 195 nuisance alligator reports. Since then the numbers have increased. In 2000 it was 280; in 2001, 320; and in

2002, there were 336 calls. According to the TPWD, in the past fifteen years, there have only been fifteen nonfatal attacks on humans by alligators. The months of April through July are the peak months for nuisance alligator calls, because spring is when gators are most active. They are looking for new territory and mates.

Houston-area game wardens use 8-by-3-foot-long rectangular metal cages that can be baited next to a pond or wherever else a nuisance gator is reported. Once caught, the gator can be winched up onto a truck or trailer. Then the gator is either relocated or killed.

Between 1972 and 1990, 127 alligator attacks against humans were reported in Florida, and five fatalities occurred. Nine fatal attacks occurred during 1970–1998, but no obvious pattern was associated with these incidents. Four of the nine fatal attacks occurred at state or county parks. In 1999 there were fifteen attacks; in 2000, twenty-three. There were seventeen attacks in 2001; fourteen in 2002; and in 2003, there was one.

More than 17 percent of injuries received by people from alligators were a direct consequence of the people intentionally touching the animal. Around the same percentage of injuries occurred while the victims were swimming. Twenty-nine percent of injuries happened when people were wading in water, snorkeling, fishing, or retrieving golf balls. People have been attacked by gators when riding in a boat, working near the water, or waterskiing. Approximately a third of all attacks are not water related. Most attacks occur in the afternoon.

Nevertheless, the risk of being attacked by an alligator is minimal not only compared to other animals, but also in relation to other water-related accidents such as scuba diving, snorkeling, boating, swimming, jetskiing, and waterskiing. No matter how slight the risk may be or how remote the chance of being attacked by an alligator, the event is typically gruesome and messy.

In 2001, alligators bit eleven people in Florida, resulting in three fatalities. In Polk County, a two-year-old girl wandered to a nearby lake from her home where she was snatched by an opportunistic alligator and drowned. A seventy-year-old man in Venice was pulled into a pond by an 8-foot-long alligator that mangled his chest, arms, and head, resulting in his death from bleeding. On Sanibel Island, near Fort Meyers, an eighty-two-year-old man was attacked as he walked his dog. The alligator bit off the man's leg from the knee down and he bled to death.

On April 21, 2004, a seventy-four-year-old woman was bitten on the leg and arm by a 10-foot-long alligator on Sanibel Island. The woman, who survived the attack, was gardening near a lake and somehow managed to fight the alligator off as it attempted to drag her into the water. The alligator was caught and destroyed.

Of thirteen fatalities documented by the FWC, only two involved males between the ages of twenty-nine and fifty-two. The rest were either elderly (age seventy or older) or children (age two to sixteen). The majority of victims were male.

The timing of 305 nonfatal attacks is also interesting. From midnight to 6:00 A.M. 20 attacks occurred, 40 from 6:01 A.M. to noon, 77 from 6:01 P.M. to midnight, and 132 from 12:01 P.M. to 6:00 P.M. The majority of attacks took place between June and August.

Even if a victim somehow manages to fight off an attacking alligator, the inflicted bites are often infected by various microbial organisms, especially gram-negative bacteria. Although seldom fatal, the resulting damage often requires a lengthy, expensive, and thoroughly unpleasant stay in a hospital.

The following chart illustrates the number of alligator attacks in the United States as of 2005. Attacks sometimes go unreported or are not recorded properly. This chart and the next one, while as up-to-date as possible, represent proportional numbers.

State	Attacks	Nuisance complaints
Florida	337	17,000
Texas	15	460
Georgia	9	400–450
S. Carolina	9	750
Alabama	5	150–250

State	Attacks	Nuisance complaints
Louisiana	2	3,000–4,000
N. Carolina	1	Undetermined
Arkansas	1	70–100
Oklahoma	0	4–6
Mississippi	0	Undetermined

The next chart depicts the number of injuries by body site. Obviously a gator attack usually includes a wound to more than one part of the body. Multiple bites are the rule rather than the exception.

Site/Percentage	Lacerations	Punctures
Hands / 53%	49	29.4
Arms / 34%	27	20.2
Legs / 32%	34	19.3
Feet/ankles / 23%	21	13.5
Torso / 14%	13	7.8
Face/head / 12%	6	5.2
Shoulder / 7%	2	2.6
Hip / 2%	2	1.4
Neck / 0%	2	0.6

Injuries to hands and arms may be defensive wounds, indicating the victim was attempting to fight back.

For eight of the reported deaths in Florida it was not known if the wounds were postmortem.

Like many other predators, alligators take the young, the old, and the overly incautious. The fact that their prey may be human and walk on two legs rather than four is not taken into consideration by the alligator.

Usually by accident, and very occasionally by design, victims of alligator attacks put themselves at risk by venturing too close to either seen or unseen alligators. Alcohol abuse and ignorance often play a major role in attacks. If not killed outright, victims usually suffer ghastly injuries. A fully grown alligator that weighs 400 pounds and has massive jaw pressure can easily take off an arm or a leg. It is an amputation with the subtlety of a dull ax.

The following incident is fairly typical of a nonfatal alligator attack on a child. While playing in a 4-foot-deep pond close to her house in Plaquermines Parish, Louisiana, on July 31, 2005, twelve-year-old Ashley Brown was suddenly bitten on one of her thighs. She tried to push the gator away, and it promptly bit her again on the hand, severing the tip of a middle finger.

The alligator refused to let go when the child attempted to get out of the water. A playmate whacked the reptile with a 2x4 piece of wood, forcing it to relinquish its grip. Relatives found the offending gator, reported to be between 7 and 8 feet long, and shot it. The victim received several skin grafts in a local hospital before being released.

■ ■ Can alligator attacks on humans be prevented? Ideally, and in theory, yes.

Exercising caution and good judgment when around, near, or in alligator habitat; respecting the animal; and having a basic knowledge of the animal should be enough to eliminate most, if not all, alligator attacks. It's not the wisest thing in the world to get too close to where alligators are, or where they're likely to be.

Here are a few simple dos and don'ts:

1 DON'T swim or wade outside of posted areas, especially at key feeding times such as dawn or dusk.

2 DON'T walk your dog along the shoreline. In essence, you're literally trolling him, using him as bait, and if there

are alligators in the vicinity it will surely arouse their curiosity and trigger a response.

3 DON'T disturb active nests. Remember that the very protective mother is always nearby even if you can't see her.

4 DO stay alert at all times. Alligators are extremely adept at concealing themselves under the water until the last possible moment, and can propel themselves out of the water like an intercontinental ballistic missile from a Trident submarine.

5 DON'T feed alligators. They will associate man with food and lose their fear of man.

6 DO teach children to respect alligators and watch them all the time when in alligator habitat.

7 NEVER charge an alligator or try and bluff it.

8 NEVER throw anything at an alligator except as a defensive measure.

9 DO yield the right of way to an alligator and give it as wide a berth as possible.

10 DO avoid the tail if faced with a contact. It can be a powerful weapon.

11 DON'T harass or molest alligators.

12 DO dispose of fish scraps in garbage cans.

13 DON'T let your pet swim in alligator-posted waters.

Is it realistic to think that most people will follow all of the above suggestions? Probably not. For reasons known only to them, otherwise relatively intelligent people will continue to tempt fate when near alligators. Whether it's out of ignorance, bravado, or a weird and misplaced sense of ego fulfillment, a small number of individuals will get bitten, and unfortunately, a number of those will die. (Children are the obvious exception to this "rule," since they don't possess the same levels of knowledge or experience as adults. Nearly half of all known human fatalities were youngsters under the age of twelve.)

Some people have uncomfortably close encounters with alligators and suffer no physical harm whatsoever; others pass close to the reptiles without even being aware of their presence. The safest course of action is to be cautious at all times.

CHAPTER FOUR

COMMERCIAL USES: FARMING AND RANCHING

■ ■ Alligators are in essence a natural, renewable resource that can be exploited for financial gain and profit. Requiring little maintenance, gators are reptilian cash cows that annually pump millions of dollars into several states' economies.

The issuance of various licenses, nuisance control programs, and their associated alligator cullings are only part of the total revenues that states derive from alligators. Farming—or *captive breeding*, as it is sometimes called—is a huge income generator for states that have sizeable alligator populations.

American alligators were systematically hunted for their hides at the start of the nineteenth century. By the end of the century the annual harvest was about 150,000 per year. The alligator population was subsequently decreased by habitat loss and overharvesting.

By the 1950s the population had severely declined, and by the 1960s, in recognition of the precipitous depreciation in numbers, most states banned hunting. As a result, alligators were classified as either en-dangered or threatened by the 1971 Endangered Species Act, thus pro-tecting them from further exploitation. Alligator population recovery was swift and dramatic, particularly in Louisiana, which had banned harvests since 1962. Ten years later the state allowed limited harvesting. Under federal protection most other southern states experienced alliga-tor population increases.

In 1983 the U.S. Fish and Wildlife Service changed the classification of the American alligator under the Convention on International Trade in Endangered Species of Wild Fauna and Flora (CITES) to "threatened for reasons of similarity in appearance," which meant that the sale of al-ligator hides and meat must be strictly regulated (tags, markings, and documentation), so that similar crocodilian species that are threatened and/or endangered in other parts of the world are not sold illegally as American alligators.

In 1991, 125,357 harvested alligators (or 77.8 percent of the total harvest) came from farms and/or ranches. A farm is defined as a closed breeding facility that doesn't depend on getting eggs or animals from the wild. A ranch uses wild-caught stock. Eggs and hatchlings form the basis of rearing enterprises. Quotas decide how many adults can be taken, and their hides are traded under stringent guidelines.

In Louisiana capitalization is primarily in the form of egg collection for ranches, and a managed hunt that utilizes seasonal habitat isolation of female alligators into less-accessible parts of the range. This focuses the hunt on males, which account for 65 to 75 percent of the harvest.

Wild harvest generates between 20,000 to 25,000 skins annually, but farm-produced skins number between 88,000 to 150,000 per year (on average, five times as many), bringing in a total of $19,272,353. When another $3.4 million is added for meat, the total economic im-pact for farm-produced alligators is $23,639,928—which is a tidy sum of money for any state's coffers.

Egg collection from private- and state-owned lands yields between 150,000 to 250,000 eggs annually, which are then distributed to farms (or ranches, as they are often called). Seventeen percent, or between 35,000 to 40,000 of the alligators commercially ranched (longer than 1.2 meters or 3.94 feet), are required to be returned to the wild, replenishing alligator populations and ensuring that there will never be a shortage.

Alligators are, at least in Louisiana, an ongoing and extremely cost-effective resource. There are currently sixty-four farms holding more than 500,000 alligators. As with any farming enterprise, the emphasis is on a controlled environment that will yield maximum growth. About 75 percent of all wild alligator hides and 85 percent of all farmed hides used by tanners around the world come from Louisiana. Gators are obviously big business in the Pelican State.

Florida first used alligators commercially in the 1880s. Unregulated hunting led to a severe depletion of populations well into the 1960s, and they did not begin to rebound until the alligator's classification under the Endangered Species Act. Eggs as well as hatchlings are also collected in Florida. Harvest allocations are based on annual population surveys and nest counts. Studies demonstrate that alligator populations remain stable when up to 13 percent of animals over four feet long are hunted annually, or up to 50 percent of located nests are collected for ranching.

There are around thirty alligator farms in Florida that generate over 15,000 hides a year, and approximately 300,000 pounds of meat annually. Prices of hides varies (the average is around $25 a foot), but meat generally sells in the $5- to $7-per-pound range. In 2002, ranches produced 207,727 pounds of meat and 140,662 feet of hides from 27,473 skins, for an estimated total commercial value of $3,941,416.

Revenues realized from alligator ranching not only support habitat maintenance, but also create a multitude of manufacturing jobs. Alligator ranches and their associated jobs are typically located in somewhat isolated rural areas where the unemployment rate tends to run higher than in the more-developed parts of the state.

Sustainable use of alligators in the United States produces more than $60 million annually, providing a considerable inducement to retain habitat and accept alligators. Fees from the regulatory system provide funding for management, regulation, enforcement, and research programs on alligators. Texas has a small program; and in 2001, the South Carolina General Assembly approved a somewhat unusual plan to both jump-start and sustain an alligator ranching program.

Poultry production is the number-one farm activity in South Carolina, where diligent chicken and turkey farmers produce more than 200 million birds per year. Around 3 percent of the birds die before they make it to market, and that translates into around 37 million pounds of carcasses that are currently composted, burned, buried, or turned into dog food (and other products probably best left unmentioned). The state's plan involves feeding these dead birds to alligators in newly created farms. However, because of the alligator's current status in South Carolina (it's illegal to catch alligators in the wild or to take their eggs), they would have to be imported from other states. The idea has not yet been signed into law.

According to the Florida Department of Agriculture and Consumer Services, Bureau of Seafood and Aquaculture, in 2000 the estimated wholesale producer values for Florida alligator meat was over $8.5 million. The retail value was considerably higher. More than 30 percent of all the alligator income in Florida comes from the sale of meat.

When compared to other meats such as beef, chicken, and fish, farm-raised alligator is low in fat and calories and high in protein. The chart below outlines the nutritional breakdown of four ounces (110 grams) of raw alligator meat:

		Percent of Daily Value
Calories	110	
Calories from fat	20	
Total fat	2g	3%
Saturated fat	0.5g	4%
Cholesterol	55 mg	18%
Sodium	55 mg	3%

		Percent of Daily Value
Total carbohydrate	0g	0%
Dietary fiber	0%	0%
Sugars	0%	0%
Protein	24 g	

It's anybody's guess how many people are whipping up sautéed alligator medallions in Dijon mustard sauce, or crocked gator ribs, but it's hard to argue with the $8.5 million they spend. The *New York Times* reported that alligator was on the menu at the Explorer's Club 100th anniversary dinner held in March 2004 at the Waldorf-Astoria Hotel in New York.

It's also hard to argue with the natural beauty of products made from alligator hides, whether it's ladies' handbags or gentlemen's cuff links. The items are typically sold in upscale markets, and while gender-segregated to an extent—purse items such as compacts, mirrors, perfume atomizers, bracelets, and necklaces for the gals, and boots, hat bands, and wide, heavy-buckled belts for the guys—all have equal appeal to both males and females because of the uniqueness and durability of each item.

The single most distinguishing feature of alligator leather is the umbilical scar; the alligator is the only crocodilian that has this feature. It may take as many as three belly sections to make a single purse.

There are other differentiating characteristics between alligators, crocodiles, and caimans, such as the head bump rows on the back of the head (2-2-2, 4-2, and 4-4-2 respectively), and the scale patterns (an alligator's is slightly less even than a crocodile's, while a caiman's is elongated), but the average consumer probably won't be able to tell the difference; and even if they could, more than likely, they wouldn't care.

Like any other in-demand product that has a high retail value, alligator hides invite counterfeiting. Are caimans being passed off as alligators to unsuspecting buyers? Or worse, are highly threatened or endangered species of crocodiles being sold as alligators, or blatantly smuggled into the United States? Probably.

The success and profitability of legal trade often promotes illegal trade. As long as there are extreme differences in income levels and qualities of life, people in developing or third-world countries will do just about anything to survive. If that includes killing endangered species . . . well, people on the short end of life's stick tend to do what they have to do.

The beauty of tanned and polished alligator hides notwithstanding, alligator farms do have their dirty little secrets. It takes between twelve to eighteen months under strict farming practices and guidelines for alligators to reach a harvest size of four to five feet. In the wild, it would take four to five years to reach the same length.

Alligator farms are no different than any other business where you have to move inventory in order to maintain the desired profit level. The longer inventory is kept in-house, the more expenses are incurred by the manufacturer. The idea, perfected by the Japanese (auto and truck manufacturers like Honda and Toyota) is to have few or no items in stock, thereby eliminating overhead costs. Demand dictates productivity. Once demand is established, increased waiting time invariably creates more demand.

If this can't be accomplished, the next best thing is to move merchandise from the manufacturer to the consumer as quickly as possible, thus reducing overhead expenses and maximizing profits. In essence, it makes no difference if the commodity is an alligator or a truck—the principle is the same. Customers are obviously anxious to buy huge amounts of alligator meat and hides, so the most cost-efficient thing to do is to move alligators through the hatchling-to-hide process as quickly as possible. It's supply and demand, profit versus loss—and time always equates into money.

Farmed alligators are fed as much as they can eat, and a relatively simple formula dictates how much and exactly what an alligator has to be fed in order to make it grow a predetermined number of inches or feet within an optimum period of time—and how much it will cost. The alligator-hide business more than quadrupled between 1987 and 1995, yielding more than 200,000 hides in 1995. There is a great deal of money and many jobs created and sustained by the alligator-hide industry. This trickles down to the the tanners, cutters, and dyers in the factories, and ultimately, to the craftspeople who make inlaid perfume atomizers, boots, shoes, watchbands, and more.

All those individuals associated with alligator hides are subsequently employed by various manufacturers. Everyone—starting with the trapper who collects the eggs or juvenile alligators and trucks them to the farm, and ending with the individual consumer who buys a pair of alligator shoes or a watchband—pays a huge amount of collective taxes.

A cursory Internet search revealed a site selling men's boots made from natural alligator: $397 (reduced from $599), and $1,227 (reduced from $1,595). The same site also advertised boots made from crocodile, ostrich, rattlesnake, python, and shark skin. Another site advertised men's shoes made from crocodile, crocodile/ostrich, and crocodile/anaconda skins ranging in price from $399 to $595. A pair of shoes made from baby alligator skin was listed at $695. From hatchling to a $700 pair of shoes, in approximately a year and a half.

A Canadian site offered ladies' purses for sale, from (in U.S. dollars) $575 to a decadent $2,970, and ladies' wallets, from $150 to $430. Men's belts sell for $240. The site's advertising copy contains the following: "These handmade articles are made with real natural crocodile. Products marked out by the 'Ligator' trademark do not contain any components that can be easily identified of animals included in the CITES Appendix I and II." The advertising copy goes on to say that the components are not part of an endangered species. The word *crocodile* seems to mean *alligator* here. Alligator belts for men on another site sell for $350.

When you compare the extremely low cost of raising alligators with the final retail cost of items made from their hides, alligator farming is almost a reptilian license to print money. Even if you have to incubate the eggs, provide extremely basic housing for unskilled labor (making at best slightly above minimum wage), and provide food for the alligators for eighteen months (until slaughter time)—it's still an incredibly profitable industry.

The alligator-hide industry spawns a multitude of other industries, including meat-packing plants, packaging facilities, and more, which keep spinning off, so gross amounts that reflect what the industry is worth to each state are probably conservative. What is not included in the gross amounts are the additional tax revenues gained from the jobs that are created, and the reduction in the number of individuals who might otherwise be on public assistance. More jobs eliminate the associated costs to the federal and state governments in terms of food stamps, welfare payments, and state-financed reduced health costs and telephone and utility bills.

However, as with any industry where time equals money, either lost or gained, shortcuts are sometimes taken, and less-than-satisfactory practices are not entirely unknown. Some people are bothered more than others.

The Animal Liberation Front (ALF), characterized by the federal government as a "special-interest extremist group," has not yet gotten involved with alligator farming, but People for the Ethical Treatment of Animals (PETA) has. No matter what your opinion of PETA is (and many consider them to be extremists in their zealotry), they nevertheless bring disturbing aspects of alligator farming to our attention.

On farms, young alligators may be kept in tanks above ground, while the larger reptiles live in pools half-submerged into concrete slabs. According to Florida's regulations, as many as 350 6-foot alligators may legally inhabit a space the size of a typical family home (although the size of the home is not specified).

Alligators on farms may be beaten to death with hammers and axes, sometimes remaining conscious and in agony for up to two hours after being skinned.

According to PETA, in one (unspecified) farm, the practice of bludgeoning and knifing alligators is not uncommon. Once removed to a killing area, workers armed with metal (probably aluminum) baseball bats proceed to bludgeon the alligators' heads, often multiple times. As the alligators struggle to flee, workers stab the animals' necks with knives.

Shooting with a .22 caliber rifle can often cause splintering of the skull, thus contaminating some neck and jowl meat. A neck nape stab-and-pith method is often used instead. A worker stands on the alligator's head and a wet, heavy material is placed over the alligator's eyes to calm the animal and prevent it from seeing what is about to happen. A sharp chisel is then forced between the base of the skull and the first vertebra, to stun the animal. Once stunned, a rod of about 3mm in diameter is used to probe and destroy the brain. Often unproductive, makeshift devices such as hammers and chisels are used; and sometimes, five or six blows are needed to sever the spinal cord. Although unable to move around, some (if not many) alligators may still be alive and semi-conscious when skinning begins. Alligators feel pain.

Clearly, no one expects abattoirs or places of slaughter to be Club Meds; however, descriptions of their daily activities should not contain litanies of horror and torture. Even taking PETA's hyperbole into consideration, alligator farms are places where it is highly likely, and even probable, that animal cruelty is the norm rather than the exception.

The purpose of alligator farms, like any other business, is to make money. State laws that govern farms take into consideration many different factors and formulate regulations that meet and satisfy as many needs as possible. However, PETA's screedy rhetoric not withstanding, the only instrument that will force change (if indeed, change is necessary) is a vociferous outcry from the general public, and so far it has not been forthcoming.

PETA's in-your-face tactics may not work all the time, but they do serve to raise public awareness. Alligators in an unspecified McDonald's in an unspecified city in Orange County, Florida, were put on display along with turtles. After PETA made a complaint to the Department of Professional Regulations, the display was removed. An alligator wrestling show at the Riverside County Fair and National Date Festival in Indio, California, was closed in 2000 after PETA claimed the show was an illegal display that violated California's animal cruelty laws.

PETA is not the only organization raising awareness. In May of 2002, Germany's parliament voted to give animals constitutional rights. Over 540 members of parliament voted in favor of the amendment to the country's fifty-three-year-old constitution, which includes protection of animals. Although it was essentially a symbolic gesture, it nevertheless gave new moral weight to the rights of animals.

New York Environmental Conservation Law CLS ECL 11-0536 prohibits the sale of certain wild animals or wild animal products. Alligators are included in the law. The Washington state legislature is considering House Bill 1151, which would ban the private possession of dangerous animals such as tigers, pumas, lions, bears, wolves, alligators, and nonhuman primates.

The California Senate is considering a bill (SB 1207) that would overturn the current state law that prohibits the sale or import of body parts from alligators, crocodiles, and other animals such as sea otters, jaguars, cheetahs, sea turtles, and wolves. SB 1207 is supported by the Fur Commission and opposed by PETA, the Humane Society of the United States, and the Fund for Animals, among other groups.

On Earth Day, April 22, 2003, representatives from the California Department of Fish and Game arrested the owner of Tiger Rescue in Glen Avon, Riverside County, on charges of animal cruelty. In addition to tigers and two alligators, other exotic animals were being kept in appalling conditions.

Metro Animal Services of Louisville, Kentucky, forced Wet Willy's, a dance club, to cancel plans to put a pit of live alligators under a glass dance floor. In December 2000, a nine-year-old boy was arrested by police after he threw a rock at an alligator in the Honolulu Zoo. The alligator received slight injuries to his face and the boy was ordered to attend counseling services with his parents. No doubt there are countless other examples of cruelty toward alligators and other crocodilians.

Applicable laws are being enforced. However, animal control agencies are often undermanned, and agents are burdened with an impossibly heavy workload, reducing their effectiveness and in essence enabling those who would perpetrate cruel acts upon alligators and crocodilians. Unfortunately, there are no laws against exercising poor judgment, and there's no doubt that certain individuals will continue to keep alligators as pets or display items.

BIG CITY ALLIGATORS FROM NEW YORK TO SCOTLAND

■ ■ One of the great urban legends of all time is the fable about alligators in New York City sewers, which goes something like this: New Yorkers return from their Florida vacations with baby alligators. They soon find their new pets have grown too large, so they promptly flush the gators down their toilets, where they wind up in the city sewers. Like all myths, this one does have a grain of truth in it. Two small boys produced a dead 36-inch-long alligator they found near the Bronx River on June 30, 1932. Police concluded that it was someone's pet.

On February 10, 1935, sixteen-year-old Salvatore Condulucci and some friends, all residents of East 123rd Street near the Harlem River, were shoveling snow into an open manhole when they discovered a large alligator lurking in the black slush ten feet below the street level. After lassoing the reptile and dragging it out of the manhole, they attacked it with shovels, killing the creature. The carcass was brought to the Lehigh Stove and Repair Shop, where it measured 7.5 to 8 feet in length, and weighed 125 pounds.

At 9:00 P.M. that night, a Department of Sanitation truck took the alligator away. Its final destination was an incinerator located on Barren Island. It was theorized that the alligator fell overboard from a passing steamer coming from the Everglades, swam toward shore, and found the entrance to the conduit. Another 150 yards through melting snow brought it to the open manhole.

Two years later on May 31, a barge captain on the East River spotted a 4-foot-long alligator, and it too was assumed to have come off a boat en route from the South.

Another escaped pet, a 26-inch-long alligator, was spotted in a Westchester County, New York, reservoir in August 1982, and in July of 1997, a 4-foot alligator was captured in Central Park.

A small (18- to 24-inch) spectacled caiman was seen in Central Park's Harlem Meer, a small lake in the northeastern section of the park, on Saturday, June 16, 2001, and was captured five days later by an alligator wrangler imported from Florida. Dubbed "Damon the Caiman" by parks commissioner Henry Stern, the reptile was temporarily housed in the Central Park Zoo until more permanent arrangements could be made.

In September of 2003, a 3-foot-long alligator was captured in Blue Heron Park, Staten Island, New York, and was turned over to animal control officers. The reptile had been living in the lake for several months, and authorities said it was an illegal pet dumped by its owners.

■ ■ Although New York City's sewer system consists of 6,000 miles of tunnels and is replenished every day with a billion gallons of water, in reality, the sewers are too polluted, cold, and dark to sustain an alligator for very long. While rats (which alligators eat) are rampant, so are alligator-killing diseases.

There are 63 million households in the United States that have pets, and about 4 million own reptiles. The crocodilian percentage has been too small to register on the American Pet Products Manufacturers Association biannual survey, but dealers estimate that several thousand Americans own alligators.

For many people, the presence of existing laws and zoning and/or animal ordinances prohibiting the ownership of alligators and other crocodilians are not enough to deter ownership. Fines are typically small, culprits rarely go to jail, and it is all too easy to abandon or dump an alligator or other crocodilian when they get too large. Thus, the alligator pet trade is alive and well.

Alligators can easily be bought on the Internet. Anyone with a computer and an ISP or access to them can buy crocodilians. One particularly odious site sells baby alligators for $100, 12- to 16-inch-long alligators for $125, and 18- to 24-inch-long alligators for $150. The site claims to have Nile crocodiles and dwarf caimans for sale as well. The same site is filled with numerous fallacies, including the statements that alligators can live for more than 100 years, and can go for more than one year if necessary without food. The site also declares that alligators are protected because "the government makes millions of dollars a year off taxes from alligators, just as most reptiles in the wild, unless the state can make money off them they are protected."

A buyer searching the Internet will not lack for choices of sites. Irresponsible traffickers are all too numerous and eager to sell their wares. Complete how-to books and pamphlets can also be downloaded free of charge from the Internet. Numerous sites originate in the United Kingdom. Some sites go into great detail and list current prices of all available crocodilians.

In addition to alligators, dwarf and spectacled caimans are touted as viable alternatives because of their relatively small size, falsely implying that they are easier to handle and manage. All of the crocodilian species, despite their international status, are discussed in great detail and ranked according to their suitability.

Under the guise of providing information, these misguided entrepreneurs subtly promote the growing (and in many instances, illegal) pet trade in alligators, caimans, and other crocodilians. By increasing the demand, irresponsible dealers under the guise of free enterprise also aid, abet, and encourage poaching and smuggling of endangered species.

When they raided a house in Rhondda, Wales, in October 2001, the Royal Society for the Protection of Cruelty to Animals inspectors found a 2-and-a-half-foot-long caiman. The Federation of British Herpetologists reported that two years earlier in December 1999, RSPCA officers rescued a 5-foot-long American alligator from an apartment in Chesterfield, where it had been living in a plastic pond liner in a 10-foot-square bedroom. The animal had been imported from the United States to live in a local zoo, was subsequently sold to a pet shop, and later bought by an exotics collector. The new owner, who did not have a Dangerous Wild Animal permit, was unable to cope with the gator.

Usually the first time an alligator or caiman chomps on its owner's arm will also be the last. Many crocodilian pets are dumped, further burdening local animal control agencies and putting an unsuspecting public at potential risk.

Customs agents at major air and sea ports of entry, such as Miami International Airport and the Port of Miami, are overworked and understaffed. Other designated U.S. ports for wildlife are Atlanta, Baltimore, Boston, Honolulu, Los Angeles, Newark, Portland, San Francisco, Chicago, Dallas/Fort Worth, New Orleans, New York, and Seattle.

Profits from the illegal and/or exotic pet trade that includes crocodilians are enormous. For every endangered crocodilian that is discovered, many more remain undetected, inevitably making their way through the chain of buyers and sellers, to eventually wind up in the possession of uncaring and often ignorant buyers.

The reasons why an individual would want an alligator, caiman, or other crocodilian as a "pet" are complex and myriad. Clearly, they cannot be trained. At best they become used to the presence of humans, which is often mistaken for acceptance or affection. They are also totally reliant upon their human owners for food.

Once they reach a size of 4 to 5 feet, alligators, crocodiles, caimans, and gharials are extremely dangerous. Just because they accept food from an owner does not mean they would stop themselves from eating their possessor in the blink of a vertical-slitted eye. No doubt there's a certain mystique associated with owning a crocodilian. Perhaps these exotic pets fill a certain egotistical need in their owners. All things considered, most people would be better served with having a dog for a pet. They don't call them Fido ("faithful" in Latin) for nothing!

CHAPTER SIX

HUNTING GATORS: RULES AND REGS

■ ■ Alligators are legally hunted in several states. The meat can be eaten (it really does taste like chicken—no joke!—as does rattlesnake) or sold, and the hides can be merchandised as well. Heads are either stuffed or reduced to the bare skull. (Ants do the cleaning; they take a while, but are amazingly thorough.) Other body parts are utilized in the form of novelty items such as back scratchers, key chains, paperweights, etc., for sale in souvenir shops.

The Guide to Alligator Hunting in Georgia is relatively representative of hunting regulations enforced by other states. Here's an excerpt:

> Both the bangstick (a shotgun shell on the end of a stick) and the handgun should be aimed at the brain, angled slightly forward from the rear of the skull. Hunters should note that the improper placement and discharge of the handgun or bangstick can occasionally only knock the alligator temporarily unconscious. . . . Harpoons or

gigs may be used for attaching a restraining line to an alligator. Harpoons or gigs consist of a penetrating point such as a straightened fish hook, detachable dart, fish gig or spear point that is attached to a restraining line. The harpoon point is typically mounted on a pole, arrow shaft or spear and is thrown. A gig (a pronged instrument with a metal or wooden pole) is jabbed.

In Georgia and other states, alligators are hunted at night from a boat, and the powerful beam from a light is used to reveal the red-eye shine. Once spotted, the gators are then captured and pulled close to the boat, where they are killed.

Florida has county-wide harvests, and the Florida Fish and Wildlife Conservation Commission publishes the following guidelines:

> Participants may take alligators using hand-held snares, harpoons, gigs and snatch hooks; manually operated spears, spearguns, crossbows and bows with projectiles attached to a restraining line and baited; wooden pegs less than two (2) inches in length attached to a hand-held restraining line. The use of baited hooks, gig-equipped bangsticks, or firearms for taking alligators is prohibited, except that bangsticks are permitted for taking alligators attached to a restraining line.

Each person issued a permit is allowed to take two nonhatchling alligators. Airboats and outboard motor–driven boats are regulated by local or regional governments.

Because alligators produce much-needed revenue, states are vigorous in their enforcement of existing laws. The Louisiana Department of Wildlife and Fisheries regulations state that: "No fur trapper, alligator hunter or fur dealer shall transport or ship raw furs or alligator skins out of the state without first obtaining an official out-of-state shipping tag from the Department."

There is a severance tax of two cents ($.02) for each alligator skin taken within the state. Skins used for personal use are subject to a $4.25 hide tag fee. Hunting season is usually from the first week of September to the first week of October.

Enforcement of existing regulations can have punitive results. On September 1, 2004, Louisiana enforcement agents cited two Assumption Parish alligator hunters (Tommy Aucoin and Johnny Hendrix, both thirty-one) for allegedly possessing untagged gators in Lafourche Parish. The suspects had five alligators in their boat, three of which were not tagged. Failing to tag gators upon taking them carries a penalty of up to $750 in fines, jail for up to 120 days, or both.

Three men were cited for taking an alligator in closed season. Elgin Floyd, Frederick Hanchett, and Randy Hanchett, all in their mid-twenties, had a 6.5-foot-long gator in their boat. The gator was seized and sold.

Betty Davis, forty-three, thought having an alligator for a pet was a good idea. Enforcement division agents thought otherwise, and cited the Amelia (St. Mary Parish) resident for possessing a live alligator without having a permit. She faced fines of $250 to $500, a jail term of no more than ninety days, or both.

On March 19, 2004, Andrew Zar, twenty-one, and Archie Enclade, sixty-six, of Lafitte in Jefferson Parish, were arrested and cited, both for taking an alligator during closed season and for illegally possessing an alligator. In Enclade's home, agents found two pounds of alligator meat in the refrigerator, along with a 4-foot-long recently killed and skinned alligator. Both men were promptly booked into the Jefferson Parish Correction Center. The alligator was valued at $140.

■ ■ ■

Danny Ware, thirty-six, Daniel Ware, eighteen, and Jeremy Green-
lee, twenty-seven, were cited on November 24, 2005, for taking
gators without a license, and in a closed season. Agents observed
them throwing a 3-foot-long gator over the side as their boat approached the boat launch at the Three Rivers Wildlife Management
Area in Avoyelles Parish. The men were also in possession of one
raccoon. It is illegal to take raccoons from a boat and without the
aid of a dog. They faced fines totaling $1,750, plus jail time of up to
ninety days, or both—plus court costs.

Ville Platte resident Billy Foreman, twenty-nine, thought no one
would notice that he had a 9-foot-alligator in the back of his truck.
A St. Landry Parish sheriff's deputy stopped him and notified LDFW
agents, who seized the alligator and later returned it to the wild.
Foreman faced fines of $400 to $750, plus jail time of up to ninety
days (or both), plus court costs.

In addition to the levied fines, licenses and their associated taxes are
also an excellent source of state revenue.

CHAPTER SEVEN

CROCODYLUS ACUTUS: AN AMERICAN ORIGINAL

■ ■ A true crocodile was first discovered in Florida in 1875 when a pair of specimens was collected in Arch Creek at the head of Biscayne Bay. One hundred years later they were listed on the endangered species list in the United States. They have been protected by the state of Florida since 1950.

Key Largo and extreme southern Florida lie within the northernmost range of the American crocodile. The species can also be found in isolated estuaries of Jamaica (where it is part of the Jamaican coat of arms); in Hispaniola, Cuba (including the Isla de la Juventud); the Caymans (Little Cayman and Cayman Brac); and along the eastern coast of Mexico, from the Bay of Campeche south, through the offshore islands of Belize, to Venezuela, Costa Rica, Nicaragua, Panama, and Colombia.

On the Pacific Coast, it is found from Sinaloa, Mexico, and the Tres Marias Islands, south to coastal Ecuador and the Rio Chira in Peru. It is the most widely distributed of the four crocodiles present in the New

World. The estimated wild population is 10,000 to 20,000. In Mexico, Belize, and Guatemala, it shares its range with Morelet's crocodile.

The broad-snouted Morelet's crocodile (*C. moreletii*) maxes out at around 12 feet, making it the smallest of the New World crocs. Although it can be found in some areas of brackish water, it prefers freshwater lagoons, swamps, ponds, and marshes. It is the only New World croc that is a solely mound-nesting species.

The Morelet's crocodile has been exploited for its hide, reducing its estimated wild population to between 10,000 and 20,000. The International Union for Conservation of Nature and Natural Resources (IUCN) Red List has it as "Low Risk, Conservation Dependent." However, robust populations exist in some areas of Mexico, such as the Centla Biosphere Reserve, the Sian Ka'an Biosphere Reserve, and the Lacandon forest.

Captive breeding programs have been initiated in Belize. The Cox Lagoon Sanctuary on the 36,077-acre Singh Tut Big Farm is around 28 miles west of Belize City and extends 3.5 miles from Cox Creek to Mussel Creek. The open freshwater of Cox Lagoon is surrounded by swamp forest, and on the western side there is a vast sweep of marsh. In Sinaloa on the Pacific coast of Mexico, a request to record a captive breeding facility for international trade was approved in 1996 by the CITES Secretariat.

The Cuban crocodile (*C. rhombifer*) can be found on the offshore island of Isla de la Juventud (in Lanier Swamp, where their predicted extermination is due to the introduction of the common caiman), and the isolated Zapata Swamp in the northwest. Because of its meager and limited distribution, it is the most threatened New World crocodilian species. The principal dangers to indigenous populations are hunting, habitat loss, the hybridization with American crocs, and predation of the young by the introduced brown caiman. The IUCN classifies this species as "Endangered." The estimated wild population is 3,000 to 6,000.

Cuban crocs are fairly large, with an average size of 12 feet, and a maximum of around 16 feet. They are considered by those who work with them to be arguably the most dangerous species of all because of their lightning-fast speed. They attack with little or no provocation and can also attack in packs.

In the United States, crocodile habitat is protected in the Crocodile Lake National Wildlife Refuge in North Key Largo, the Everglades National Park, Biscayne National Park, J. N. "Ding" Darling National Wildlife Refuge on Sanibel Island in southern Lee County, Collier Seminole State Park in Collier County, and Key Largo Hammocks State Botanical Preserve. Isolated crocodiles manage to survive in remnant mangrove habitats in several Miami-Dade County parks, including Matheson, Snapper Creek, Black Point, Chapman Field, and Crandon.

Although they are somewhat similar in appearance to alligators, the American crocodile has needs specific to its species. The most important limiting nesting factor is the availability of brackish water. Nurseries need slightly salty water. Water found in the Gulf of Mexico and the Atlantic Ocean is too saline.

Coastal mangrove swamps with their entanglements of exposed root systems not only provide suitable hiding places for hatchlings, but they also trap nutrient-rich sediment. The sediment in turn supports other animals, including crocodile prey. They also provide the crocodiles protection from strong offshore winds. Burrows are often dug 10 to 30 feet into creek beds, with entrances at or below the waterline.

Females reach sexual maturity between 10 to 13 years of age, and breeding begins in April. Successful nests of excavated soil are usually located at the edge of a saltwater marshland. Nests are low mounds up to 2 feet tall, and can be 20 feet in diameter. Eggs are subject to predation by raccoons, birds, and snakes.

Hatching occurs during July and August after approximately eighty-five days of incubation. As with alligators, temperature determines sex. Eggs incubated between 91 and 93 degrees Fahrenheit produce only females, while those incubated below 87 degrees will produce mainly females.

Baby crocodiles are vulnerable to predation by raccoons, blue crabs, other crocodilians, and birds, such as ibis, gulls, herons, hawks, and eagles.

Their mortality rate is extremely high, with only about 10 percent of hatchlings surviving their first year. A newborn crocodile can live for more than four months without eating by using the fat from the remains of the yolk sac stored in its belly. Aquatic and terrestrial larvae are the favorite food of hatchlings, but they will also eat anything else they can catch. Hatchlings are a yellowish tan to gray with dark cross markings.

After hatching, young crocodiles immediately take shelter in the nurseries, displaying almost identical behavior to similarly aged and sized alligators. If the crocodiles survive their first year and reach a length of 16 to 20 inches, they, like their alligator cousins, will be capable of consuming former predators.

The crocodile population in the United States is slowly increasing. Estimates put the number at between 500 and 1,000. Crocodiles will adapt to noise and boat traffic. In some areas, like the Crocodile Lake National Refuge in North Key Largo, three to four subadults and adults wind up as roadkill each year. Crocodiles also perish during occasional summer tropical storms and hurricanes that make landfall in extreme South Florida. Tidal surges, rough seas, and high winds presumably cause deaths, and can damage nests and vital nesting beaches. In addition, these weather-related forces often unfavorably modify habitat features.

While on assignment for *Reptiles* magazine, I met with Steve Klett, manager of the Crocodile Lake National Wildlife Refuge. Klett said, "Crocs are easy to manage. Just give them some brackish water, good nesting sites, [and some] food sources, and leave them alone. Because they're so territorial, if they're not directly threatened, they basically don't care. Just provide them with a little bit of habitat. Water quality is not an issue for adults."

Crocodiles and alligators have several characteristics in common: the approximate number and shape of their teeth; their armor-plating; their four-chambered hearts; and eye protection. In addition, they care for their young in similar ways, and they both favor opportunistic, ambush-hunting techniques.

Crocodiles don't have chemoreceptors around their jaws to locate prey, but they do have them on their body. An American crocodile's snout comes to a point (hence, *Crocodylus acutus; acutus* meaning "sharp" or "pointed" in Latin) as opposed to an alligator's rounded snout. This makes the croc's jaws more generalized and a little less powerful than those of alligators. In the water the American crocodile looks sleek and streamlined. The fourth tooth in the lower jaw is visible even when the mouth is closed, a characteristic shared by most of the world's crocodilians.

By comparison, the American crocodile is shyer than the brutish American alligator, and although 6 to 8 feet is the average size, a full-grown American crocodile can reach an eye-catching length of 15 feet (there have been unconfirmed reports of 20- and 22-foot lengths), and can tip the scales at a brawny 350 pounds.

The South American record is 23 feet, but average lengths are 8 to 12 feet. Crocodiles and gharials also differ from alligators and caimans in that they have functioning salt glands on their tongues.

CROCODILE ATTACKS

There has never been a recorded death due to a crocodile attack in the United States. Because they're so reclusive and live for the most part in remote habitats, American crocodiles—unlike alligators—haven't had as much interaction with people yet.

That's not to say the rare encounters are not hair-raising.

The Kenyons of Cape Coral, Florida, were snorkeling in the warm, clear waters near Key West's Fort Zachary Taylor State Park in 2005. Suddenly, Darren, forty-two, and Michelle, thirty-four, were startled into a stark reality they certainly weren't expecting. An alert kayaker had spotted a 5- to 6-foot-long American crocodile just yards away from the preoccupied couple, and instantly shouted a warning. Instead of watching small, brightly colored fish flitting below them, the Kenyons beheld a torpedo-long crocodile slowly cruising toward them at eyeball level.

The obviously frightened couple immediately took refuge on a tiny rock island where they prudently remained for about forty-five minutes. The reptile lost interest and eventually submerged, allowing the terrified snorkelers to make their escape.

Fatalities have occurred, however.

Sometimes it pays to stay in jail. In June 2002, Oswaldo Martinez was captured by police after fleeing to Costa Rica from Panama, where he was accused of murdering Judge Hermodio Mariscal. After escaping from prison, the suspect was eaten alive by a crocodile as he tried to swim across the River Terraba. He was trying to reenter Panama through the dense jungle that separates the two countries.

Between September 1995 and May 1998, three people were killed by American crocs in Costa Rica, where the animals are completely protected. Crocs live on both coasts, and can also be found several miles upstream in the large river systems.

The first fatal attack occurred on the Tempisque River. Since pre-Columbian times the river has offered an important mode of transportation, providing access to the Palo Verde National Park. The park boasts the most extensive variety of bird life in the country, and contains twelve different habitats, including mangroves, swamps, saltwater and freshwater lagoons, and marshes and swamp forests shared by howler monkeys, coatis, anteaters, and green iguanas.

The first incident occurred when a fisherman's small, shallow-draft boat overturned. The man attempted to swim across the river to get help—but he never made it to the other side. Large crocs also live and thrive in the Tempisque.

Another victim was also a male of unspecified age who took a swim in the invitingly cool waters of a lagoon. A croc estimated to be almost 20 feet long happened to be in the lagoon at the same time, and promptly ate the swimmer.

The third victim was a fisherman in the Jesus Maria River, who foolishly swam out to untangle a snarled fishing line and immediately fell victim to a hungry crocodile.

The Black River is the longest river in Jamaica. This scenic waterway is a favorite destination for fishers, canoeists, and nature lovers. Linda Atkinson, seventy, who owned a bar and shop in southwestern Jamaica, got into the record books in a way she'd never dreamed possible.

In 1999 Atkinson went fishing on the river's banks, hoping to catch her dinner. She became the prey when a crocodile (described by witnesses as being 10 feet long) caught her and pulled her into the river. Other fishermen at the scene bravely went to her rescue and managed to wrest her away from the croc, who was intent on making a meal of her. Sadly, Atkinson was pronounced dead at a local hospital.

Crocodiles are a protected species in Jamaica, and a major tourist attraction.

In October 1999, heavy rains deluged the homes of residents in Villahermosa, the capital of Tabasco, Mexico, causing flooding and mudslides. The streets were also inundated with water, causing much inconvenience. Crocodiles estimated at between 3 and 8 feet long sought higher ground to rest and sun themselves.

A taxi driver reported that a large croc came out into the middle of a street and blocked traffic. Soon, nine of the crocs were captured by members of the Federal Environmental Protection Agency in public parks and in heavily populated areas that were flooded. Fortunately, no one was killed by the displaced reptiles, and only one croc tried to attack a person, who did not suffer any injuries.

■ ■ ■

Six years earlier, an incident occurred near the outskirts of Puerto Vallarta, Jalisco (on the west coast of Mexico). This area is distinguished by diminutive ponds, estuaries, rivers, and impermanent wetlands, mixed with farmland tended by predominantly poor farmers.

In August an eight-year-old boy was seized by a croc around 10 feet long. The boy had been walking along a river approximately 5 feet wide by 1.5 feet deep, located just 66 feet from where the boy lived. The croc held the boy's head and left arm between its jaws. When a group of young men hit the reptile with stones and pulled its tail, the croc released the boy, who miraculously escaped with no serious wounds. Authorities speculated that the croc had escaped from the boy's house three months earlier, which explained its proximity to the house and its lack of fear of humans.

■ ■ In captivity, it's not unusual for an American crocodile to live for thirty to forty years; in the wild, its life span is obviously shorter due to food shortages, injuries from other alligators, and general hardships imposed on the animals. In North America crocodiles are outnumbered by alligators by a ratio of approximately 1,000 to 1.

The IUCN lists the American crocodile as "Vulnerable." The principal threats are illegal hunting and habitat destruction. The Endangered Species Act classifies the animal as endangered, and under the Threatened and Endangered Species Section (TESS), it is listed as a species with "Critical Habitat."

Although it has remained true to its crocodyline ancestry and heritage, the American crocodile faces specific threats caused by the same dynamics that endanger the American alligator and the Everglades.

Historically, freshwater coursing through the Everglades decreased the water's salinity where it drained into Florida Bay, creating the estuarine states that benefit crocodiles. When this natural north-to-south flow was disrupted by diverting gates, canals, and holding-pump stations, the resulting periodic big releases of freshwater into Florida Bay caused huge oscillations in the salinity levels, which changed the characteristic of the bay from estuarine to marine lagoon. These changes have a deleterious domino effect when it comes to the number and diversity of plants and animals present in the bay—many of which the crocodiles eat (in the case of animals), or, when they are young, hide among (in the case of plants).

Although there are far fewer crocs than alligators, the American crocodile is still a hardy and adaptable keynote species. Nevertheless, there comes a point when even such sturdy animals can no longer cope with the stresses they are forced to endure. Their slightly increasing population numbers are deceiving, in that the number of breeding females (estimated at twenty-five) may be too low to produce sustained and desirable population growth, especially when man-made pollutants that taint the Everglades act in evil concert with habitat loss. Has the American crocodile reached a point of no return? Probably not quite. Is it looming just over the horizon? Without a doubt.

Decline in the American crocodile's numbers was primarily due to the demand for its high-quality skin, mainly between the years 1930 to 1960. Conservation efforts are now in place throughout Central and South America.

Lastly, while crocodiles don't cry, they do produce tears, which are generated by lachrymal glands behind their eyelids, just like ours. The tears clean the eyes and help to reduce bacterial growth. Hence, the phrase "crocodile tears."

CHAPTER EIGHT

CAIMAN: DEATH SOUTH OF THE BORDER

■ ■ Caimans are found primarily in Central and South America, and most are relatively small, squat reptiles with a toothy grin. They look like smaller versions of the American alligator, and spectacled caimans are widely sold in the pet trade as baby alligators.

All of the eight species and subspecies of freshwater-dwelling caimans are in the northern parts of South America, primarily the Amazon River Basin. The Brown caiman (*Caiman crocodilus fuscus*) ranges into southern Mexico. They are the most widely distributed species in its family and inhabit almost all the low-altitude wetlands in its range.

The largest species is the black caiman (*Melanosuchus niger*, derived from *melas*—the Greek genitive for black, plus *soukhos*, Greek for "crocodile," leading to the Latin *suchus*; *niger* also means "black" in Latin). The black caiman can reach nightmare-inducing lengths of 20 feet, making it the largest caiman/alligator in the world.

The smallest caiman is the heavily-armored Cuvier's dwarf caiman (*Paleosuchus palpebrosus*) whose average length is by comparison a petite 3 to 4 feet. The estimated wild population is over 1,000,000. The IUCN Red List categorizes this species as "Low Risk, Least Concern."

The Cuvier's habitat extends through a large portion of northern South America. It can be found in Bolivia, Brazil, Colombia, Ecuador, French Guiana, Guyana, Paraguay, Peru, Surinam, and Venezuela. Because of its small size and the poor quality of its belly skin, the value of the Cuvier's hides is not very high. Threats come from habitat destruction and pollution—principally, from gold-mining enterprises.

Cuvier's dwarf caimans are collected for the pet trade, and are often sold as alligators by unscrupulous vendors to unsuspecting buyers. There is little inducement for money-making exploitation such as sustainable-yield management.

As the biggest predator in its particular ecosystem, the black caiman is a keystone species, and as such helps to maintain the structure of the ecosystem by performing such tasks as nutrient cycling and selective predation of certain fish, mammals, and other species. Like all other crocodilians, it seeks out the unwary or the unfortunate.

Caiman is a Spanish word meaning "alligator" (or any crocodilian), and although both caiman and alligators share identical behavioral and physical characteristics—such as nest building, hunting techniques, a broad nose, and brain size—there are several notable differences.

Commercial hunting for caiman skins (which produce a shiny black leather) increased dramatically during the 1940s and 1950s, as populations of other South American crocodilians were decreasing. Because it poses a danger to cattle and humans, and has stomach scales that are fairly smooth, experts estimate that during the twentieth century, 99 percent of the black caiman population has been reduced.

There are locally strong populations in Peru, Ecuador, Brazil, and Guyana, although these tend to occur in isolated areas of swampland. The species can also be found in Bolivia and French Guiana. The estimated world population is between 25,000 and 50,000. The IUCN Red List categorizes the black caiman as "Low Risk."

Even though the meat of caimans is not favored by indigenous peoples, and their hides have a low commercial value, another form of exploitation was discovered. Decomposing caiman meat is savored by the land tortoise (*Geochelone denticulata*), whose flesh is very well liked and demands a high price in regional markets. Thus, this meat is now used to bait tortoise traps. A hole is dug in the forest (approximately 3 feet deep by 1 to 1.5 feet wide at the diameter), and the hunter hangs the caiman meat above the hole. The tortoises are attracted by the smell of the rotting meat, come closer to investigate, and fall into the hole. A 5-foot-long caiman provides enough meat to bait between three and four traps, while a 2-foot-long caiman is usually used for one trap. Ten to fifteen traps are usually set by a hunter.

A rescue plan for the black caiman exists in the Peruvian Amazon, where they are trying to restrict this tortoise-hunting operation. This will likely play a role in the large-scale money-making tortoise industry in the future. Peruvian law prohibits the commercial sale of tortoises, and only permits their capture for personal use. However, in large and small cities throughout the country, hundreds if not thousands of tortoises are sold each day. By extrapolation, it can be assumed that hundreds of black caiman are being killed as a result, to use as tortoise bait.

Black caiman are exterminated from lakes by fishermen not only because the reptiles are quite dangerous when they get large, but also because they tear up the fishermen's nets. In addition to hunting, the other major threats to the black caiman are destruction of its habitat by deforestation and the burning of swamplands.

Belly scales on caiman are protected by a bony plate which renders them less valuable than other crocodilians for the hide trade, with the exception of the black caiman. Nevertheless, many caiman have been hunted for years and sold as inferior hides or skins. Usually only the flank region is used. Since the 1950s, millions of caiman have been harvested, and the common or spectacled, and the Jacaré, continue to supply the vast majority of skins on the market.

Unlike alligators, which can tolerate temperatures in the low 40s and high 30s Fahrenheit, and go into a semihibernation state, caiman do not hibernate. As a rule, caimans are nocturnal, preferring to hunt at night (some species, such as the black caiman, hunt on land). Ecological adaptability of the common caiman is evident in Florida, Puerto Rico, and Cuba, where introduced caiman populations are well established and impossible to eradicate. In certain species, such as the spectacled caiman, their average life span is demonstrably shorter in the wild. Three species of caiman (black, spectacled, and broad-snouted) have fewer teeth than alligators.

Caiman meat, although somewhat tough, can be smoked and preserved, and is a staple of many indigenous peoples. Babies and juveniles are often stuffed and sold as curios.

In Brazil's Mamiraua Sustainable Development Reserve, hunters and poachers take an estimated 100,000 tons of caiman meat, in spite of a government-permitted limited harvest. One linear inch of the black caiman, if properly tanned, can bring up to 25 U.S. dollars on the international market. In 1988 the commercial value of a legal-size, raw caiman hide at producer level in Venezuela was approximately $50. Meat sells for thirty cents a pound, and $3 will buy about a square foot of spectacled caiman hide.

The Mamiraua Reserve has arguably the greatest concentration of crocodilians anywhere in the world. Brazil's total caiman population is estimated to be in the millions. Extensive captive breeding programs are being developed, with over 100 facilities already established.

A major program in Colombia that focuses on captive breeding produces between 300,000 to 450,000 skins per year. Venezuela's caiman population is estimated at 4 million. Private hunting by landowners allows the harvesting of up to 20 percent of caiman above 5.9 feet total length each year.

The common or spectacled caiman (*Caiman crocodilus*) is named for a bony orbital ridge in front of its eyes that resembles eyeglasses. This population is healthy, and estimated at over 1,000,000. It is found in twenty countries in the Americas, including Brazil, Ecuador, El Salvador, Guatemala, Panama, Mexico, Trinidad, and the United States (as an introduced species). Hunting is typically done at night from canoes. Harpoons, rifles, shotguns, and clubs are the preferred killing methods.

Only the lateral flanks of this highly adaptable species provide skin suitable for tanning. Most of the hide market in the United States comes from the common or spectacled caiman. The skins are often passed off as alligator hides.

Of the five caiman species found in South America (the black, dwarf, Jacaré, smooth-fronted, and broad-snouted), only the black is endangered due to hunting and poaching. Populations in El Salvador and Colombia are somewhat depleted. Principal threats to all caiman are illegal hunting and habitat loss.

The broad-snouted caiman (*Caiman latirostris*) is found in northern Argentina, Bolivia, southeastern Brazil, Paraguay, and Uruguay. It is a highly aquatic species that prefers marshes, mangroves, and freshwater and brackish swamps. The estimated wild population is 250,000 to 500,000. The IUCN Red List categorizes the broad-snouted caiman as a species of "Low Risk, Least Concern."

Another species the IUCN Red List defines as Low Risk, Least Concern is the smooth-fronted caiman, also known as Schneider's dwarf caiman (*Paleosuchus trigonatus*). The estimated wild population is over 1,000,000, and is scattered throughout Bolivia, Brazil, Colombia, Ecuador, French Guiana, Guyana, Peru, Surinam, and Venezuela.

Males are relatively small (6 to 7 feet). Their osteoderm-filled skin makes this species unsuitable for commercial exploitation. Habitat destruction and pollution from gold-mining interests are the primary threats to its survival.

Caiman are being discovered in the United States because they are sold either as baby alligators or as caiman. When they get too large, irresponsible owners simply abandon them in the Everglades National Park or the Big Cypress Swamp, where they compete with the American alligator for territory and food. It is not illegal to own a caiman in Florida, but a Class II permit must be obtained.

The following chart lists caiman species, their maximum length, commercial value, and estimated wild population (the asterisk denotes subspecies). Maximum length numbers vary slightly, depending on the source.

Species	Max. Length	Commercial Value	Estimated Wild Population
Spectacled	8.2 feet	medium	over 1,000,000
Broad-snouted or Paraguayan	9.8 feet	high	250,000 to 500,000
Black	16.4–20 feet	high	25,000 to 50,000
Dwarf	7.4 feet	low	over 1,000,000
Brown*	6.5 feet	low	over 100,000
Smooth-front	8.5 feet	low	over 1,000,000

CAIMAN ATTACKS

Caiman attacks on people occur more frequently than is commonly acknowledged. During a nighttime expedition in February 1997 to catch black caiman hatchlings at Imuya Lagoon in the Rio Napo region of eastern Ecuador, an adult female caiman attempted to snatch a man who was kneeling in a canoe while grabbing caiman hatchlings.

Catching hatchlings, whether alligators or caiman, is not a particularly dangerous or complicated process. Young caiman (and alligators) do not have the fully developed lungs that will eventually allow them to submerge and surface at will. Therefore, hatchlings are more or less confined to the water's surface. The preferred and usual technique is to grab them behind the neck or by the tail and lift them into the canoe or boat.

Upon hearing her hatchlings' cries of distress, the female caiman (who is just as protective of her young as any other croco-dilian) leapt out of the water, grabbed the unfortunate man by his left buttock, inflicting painful puncture wounds, and yanked him into the dark, murky water.

After being pulled underwater to a depth of approximately 6 feet—deep enough to drown in—the victim was inexplicably released by the caiman. The terrified man surfaced and made a frantic swim for his life toward the canoe. The caiman circled ominously and attacked again. When it got close enough, a fellow expedition member whacked the reptile on its head with a wooden paddle. Whether she was discouraged or distracted, the female caiman swam away, and the victim was able to scramble back into the canoe.

In 1994 a Swiss volunteer at a national park on the Caribbean side of Costa Rica had a habit of swimming at the same place and at the same time of day, in spite of repeated warnings by park guards that a very large crocodile (caiman) was known to be present in the area. The daily swim was refreshing, and provided an excellent respite from the steamy heat and humidity that characterize the local envi-ronment. The Swiss worker, who should have known good advice when he heard it, paid with his life.

An unidentified male was killed in Guanacaste a year later, and an attack occurred near Puntarenas in 1998 when the lines on a fish-ing boat became entangled on an unknown object in the bottom of a river. Many indigenous people eke out a meager living by fishing, and it is not unusual for them to venture into caiman-infested wa-ters in search of fish.

What snagged the lines was one of several 13- to 19-foot-long caiman who were earlier seen basking on the riverbank. Deciding not to heed the warnings of his companions, the victim dove down to the bottom to unsnarl his lines. Unfortunately, he dove into the waiting, gaping jaws of a monstrously huge caiman, which proceeded to eat him.

Living as they do in often-inaccessible swamps and jungles, caiman attacks often go unreported. The indigenous human citizens of caiman habitat do not as a rule bother with detailed record keeping. Life is often cheap in these regions, and death by caiman is usually regarded as just another hazard of daily life.

ILLEGAL CAIMAN TRADE

According to CITES, illegal trade in caiman skins has been and continues to be a problem. Legal production of caiman skins now numbers in excess of half a million a year. Illegal trade undermines the economic viability and regulatory capacity of sustainable-use programs in the region. Continued enforcement within Latin America and coordinated action with the major consuming countries are needed to eliminate illegal trade in caiman skins.

The illegal or state-sanctioned trade in caiman is not confined to skins.

During a routine traffic stop in August 2004 in Edinburgh, Scotland, a man was found with a 3-foot-long spectacled caiman in the trunk of his car. The Scottish Society for the Prevention of Cruelty to Animals intervened, and the man was charged with five wildlife cruelty offenses and one count of culpable and reckless conduct.

In August 2005, a 200-pound caiman was seen sunbathing in Ken Malloy Harbor Regional Park in Los Angeles, California. According to reports, visitors to the park had repeatedly fed the animal French bread and jelly donuts as it swam in the park's 50-acre lake. The caiman was captured without incident, and now resides in the Los Angeles Zoo. Presumably its quality of life has improved, along with its diet.

A 3-foot-long caiman was ingeniously captured in May 1999 at Lake Accotink Park in Fairfax County, Virginia, with a $14 fishing net bought at a local Kmart. Park officials believe the caiman was released in the 482-acre park by someone who had been keeping the animal as a pet. When it got too large, it was released. It is legal to keep caimans as pets in Virginia if you have a state permit.

Another fishing net was used to safely corral a 3-foot-long caiman in a pond across from the Justice Center in Aurora, Colorado, in May 2002. Officials did not know how or why the caiman was in the pond. In the spring of 1986, several caiman were spotted in Green Lake in Seattle, Washington; two were captured. In August 1992, a 3-foot-long caiman was nabbed in Cottage Lake northeast of Redmond, Washington, by King County Animal Control officers.

Since 1999 trade restrictions have prevented caiman from being sold in local pet stores. However, that does not prevent them from being sold on the illegal market. Many pet store owners and their customers are unscrupulous people who do not hesitate to violate local laws in order to make a profit, or buy what they think is a cute or unusual pet.

While serving an outstanding arrest warrant on fifty-four-year-old John Calbert in January 2005, Monroe County (Michigan) police officers unexpectedly discovered a 4-foot-long caiman in the suspect's house, and seized it (along with Mr. Calbert). In Michigan, owning any animal that is not domestic to the state must be approved by the governing city or township before it can be purchased. Thus, Calbert was additionally charged with owning an illegal animal.

These are but a few of the many examples of caiman that are found in places they should never be. Not only do they pose a very real risk of injury (or even death) for their owners, but illegally released caiman (and all crocodilians) also put the usually unsuspecting general public in danger as well. The last thing a swimmer at a local park expects to find sharing the water is a large, threatening caiman. Children and dogs are especially vulnerable to attacks by all crocodilians.

The reasons why people buy these exotic pets and then foist them on an unsuspecting public are complicated and best suited for psychological studies.

■ ■ Among the most threatened crocs in the New World is the Orinoco (*C. intermedius*). It approximates the American crocodile in size and has a similar temperament. It rarely attacks without provocation. Limited distribution (Venezuela and Colombia) and lack of osteoderms—which makes the hide extremely valuable and very suitable for tanning—led to its wholesale slaughter. Significant population declines have reduced the estimated wild population to an estimated 250 to 1,500. The IUCN Red List rates the Orinoco as "Critically Endangered."

Additional threats include illegal hunting (the species is legally protected in Colombia, but this has not had an effect on poaching) and other exploitation, such as the use of meat and eggs for food; fat, feet, skulls, and teeth for medicinal purposes; the sale of young crocs in local markets; and habitat destruction in the form of deforestation. Many adult Orinocos are caught in fishing nets.

The hides of the Orinoco are very comparable to those of the American crocodile, making verification of illicit hides more difficult.

CHAPTER NINE

GATORS AND CROCS IN EUROPE: THE LAST PLACE YOU'D LOOK

■ ■ Crocodilians (mostly caiman) make unexpected appearances fairly often in places not typically associated with large, four-legged reptiles. Sightings are often accompanied by mistaken species identification, public panic that combines with a misunderstood fascination, massive local and national media coverage, and exaggeration of the animal's size.

Crocs and gators can't survive Europe's cold winters, except in zoos and the homes of people who have bought them as illegal pets. That doesn't prevent them from trying, though. No matter how factually erroneous the sightings, they are nevertheless indicative of the flourishing pet trade (much of which is illegal) in crocodilians that knows no geographical boundaries.

The highly trained divers of the Leopoldstadt fire brigade in Vienna, Austria, weren't 100 percent sure their standard-issue fire-fighting gloves would protect their hands and fingers as they attempted to corral a caiman from Vienna's Danube canal on July 19, 2001. Although the hapless reptile only measured approximately 1.3 feet, initial reports estimated its length at a physically impossible 50 feet.

Trained in water rescue, divers normally retrieved "floaters" (or drowning victims), people who had fallen into the canal by misadventure, and the occasional dog or cat. Nothing in their extensive training or collective past experience had prepared them for this particular mission.

After the successful, relatively uneventful capture, the reptile was temporarily housed in Schönbrunn Zoo, which is the oldest zoo in the world. It was founded in 1752, built in 1760, and lies in the southeastern part of the Habsburgs' summer residence. The animal was later moved to another zoo that had similar species.

A month earlier, on June 22, a 5-foot-long caiman was spotted 60 miles upstream of Eltville, which is near Wiesbaden, Germany, close to the town of Ketch in the state of Baden-Wuerttemberg. A bladder-challenged cyclist went into some bushes on the banks of the Rhine River to relieve himself, and nearly stepped on the reptile that was peacefully sunning itself on a log. The startled cyclist threw dirt and stones at the caiman, which hissed angrily and displayed a full set of sharply pointed teeth before it slithered into the river and swam away.

Four days later, accompanied by much public fanfare and media coverage, local police launched a massive croc hunt utilizing a helicopter and a patrol boat in the search for the elusive caiman. Croc experts excitedly combed the riverbanks near Eltville, where the reptile was also spotted by a barge captain who understandably thought it was a floating log. Concerned bathers were advised by local authorities to avoid the river until further notice.

The same caiman was reportedly seen two days later near Ruedeshein, 62 miles downstream. Reports of the reptile's length had increased to 10 feet by this time, and more police helicopters and patrol boats were pressed into service in an attempt to catch the elusive animal. Local croc experts agreed that in midsummer, the Rhine teems with different species of fish and birds, in addition to dogs, cats, and other pets that play on its banks. A caiman would have no difficulty in obtaining more than enough food to survive. They also agreed that a caiman was quite capable of inflicting serious—and possibly fatal—injuries to a human.

Two weeks later, after the massive search that had entailed large expenditures of the taxpayers' money failed to catch the evasive caiman, another report had the animal surfacing and menacing (or at least, swimming toward or in the general direction of) a small boat in the river.

Were people seeing things that weren't there? It's entirely possible. Floating logs are often mistaken for crocodilians, and the general public's imagination can never be accused of being conservative. The authorities concluded that the caiman was hiding in the Mariannaue nature park, and no further action was taken. If that was indeed the case, the unfortunate reptile undoubtedly froze to death either before or during the ensuing winter. It is illegal to import or keep crocodilians of any kind in Austria.

In Daisland, Sweden, on June 25 of the same year, a group of children reportedly discovered a 2-foot long dead croc in a lake named Lilla Lee. Police removed the carcass and said they had no idea where it had come from, or how it happened to wind up in a lake.

Norway's Food and Safety Authority teamed up with members of the Oslo police department to nab a 2.6-foot-long Nile crocodile that had been kept as an illegal pet in the Ulven section of the capital. The April 2005 raid ended when the owner (of the apartment where the reptile was being kept) was charged as being in violation of exotic animal regulations.

■ ■ ■

Man-made Lake Valmayor lies 10 miles northwest of the Spanish capital of Madrid. It is popular with thousands of Madrid's residents, who flock to the shores and beaches during the hot summer months in order to swim, go boating, picnic, and ten swimmers anxiously called police after seeing two large crocs in the water. One of the crocs allegedly chased a terrified swimmer out of the water. The reports were received with understandable skepticism by the authorities, until two police officers saw the reptiles for themselves.

The lake was immediately closed, and an armada of speedboats (equipped with snipers) and helicopters outfitted with heat sensors descended on the lake. Crocodile tracks were found on a beach, and two nests were discovered, which further confirmed the sightings. Traps baited with dead meat were set in an effort to catch the fugitive crocs.

Authorities surmised the reptiles had been purchased when they were very small, and when they got too big for their owners to safely handle, they were released in the lake. They were never found.

■ ■ Reinhard Reynisson, the mayor of Husavik, Iceland, investigated the possibility of using crocodiles to dispose of waste created by the town's fishing industry. The idea, floated in 2001, was inspired by a Colorado waste disposal scheme that also used crocs. As incongruous as it may sound, 100 small alligators were first brought to the tilapia fish farm in the San Luis Valley in Colorado in 1987 to dispose of dead fish and processing weight (that can be 60 percent of the whole fish weight after filleting).

The secret is a 2,050-foot-deep geothermal artesian well that conveniently provides a constant supply of water that stays at 86.9 degrees Fahrenheit year-round. In 1991, the alligators were moved to an outdoor pen that had warm water constantly flowing through it.

Six years later, the farm produced its first captive-bred gators. Twenty-four were born after incubation at 86 degrees Fahrenheit. Normally, this temperature results in females, but most of the hatchlings were male. The owners theorized that the decreased air pressure at the 9,842-foot altitude of the farm may have modified the sex-determining response, which is temperature-dependent.

In Iceland, warm, geothermal groundwater is used for domestic heating, and also, to produce electricity. In theory it is a perfect environment for crocs. Constantly warm water is one component of ideal croc habitat; a readily available supply of food is another.

In actual practice, the idea might not be so perfect, even if it did attract tourists. Although tolerant of the food they eat, crocs are very temperature-sensitive and require a relative amount of space between individuals. In Iceland they would have had to be housed in an artificially created, expensive-to-build, closely monitored environment.

Zany ideas such as this are consistently posited by people who should know better. On paper they sound innovative and creative, but in reality, they are invariably doomed to failure.

CHAPTER TEN

AFRICA'S CROCS: DEATH ON THE NILE

■ ■ The Nile crocodile is the largest of the three crocodile species found in Africa. Although they can attain a maximum length of 20 feet, most are closer to 17 feet—or about 3 feet longer than the average midsized sport utility vehicle (SUV)—and they can weigh up to approximately 1,650 pounds, or slightly less than half the weight of a midsized SUV.

Possessing bone-crushing jaw pressure, they are capable of killing large mammals such as antelope, buffalo, zebras, wildebeests, and young hippos. A human would pose no problem for a Nile crocodile, who could (and would, if given the opportunity) gobble up a grown man without even so much as a burp afterwards.

The Nile crocodile (*Crocodylus niloticus*) is among the largest and best known of all the crocodilians. *Crocodylus* is derived from the Greek *krokodeilos*, which literally means "pebble worm" (*kroko* means "pebble," and *deilos* means "worm," or "man"), and *niloticus* means "of the Nile."

These crocs are widely dispersed throughout sub-Saharan Africa, and can be found in Angola, Benin, Botswana, Burkina Faso, Burundi, Cameroon, Central African Republic, Chad, Congo, Ivory Coast, Democratic Republic of Congo, Egypt, Eritrea, Ethiopia, Equatorial Guinea, Gabon, Gambia, Ghana, Guinea, Guinea-Bissau, Kenya, Liberia, Malawi, Mali, Mozambique, Mauritania, Namibia, Niger, Nigeria, Rwanda, Senegal, Sierra Leone, Somalia, South Africa, Sudan, Swaziland, Tanzania, Togo, Uganda, Zambia, and Zimbabwe.

Historical records indicate its range formerly extended into southern Israel and Jordan. The Nile crocodile also exists on Madagascar. The estimated wild population is between 250,000 and 500,000. The IUCN rates the Nile as "Low Risk, Least Concern."

They can be found in a variety of habitats, including rivers, large lakes, and freshwater swamps. In some areas they extend down into brackish-water environments. Holes excavated in sandy banks during the annual dry season are the preferred nesting sites. Females reach sexual maturity when they reach the size of approximately 8.2 feet.

The Nile crocodile is one of the most commercially utilized species of crocodiles that produce a classic hide. In 1993, world trade numbered 80,000 skins annually, with the majority coming from Zimbabwe (54 percent) and South Africa (15 percent), from ranching and captive breeding. The Nile crocs seen basking on riverbanks are identical to the ones the ancient Egyptians raised to the status of living gods, thousands of years before the birth of Christ.

However, twenty-first-century Nile crocs are more man-eaters than gods. Wherever they are found they are rightfully regarded as the top predator. Feared and respected, these reptiles use a combination of stealth, jaw pressure (measured in the thousands of pounds per square inch), and sheer bulk to subdue their prey.

The Kunene River courses into Namibia from Angola in the north and slashes a deep, slender trough in the otherwise arid landscape of Kaokoland. The river terminates its journey to the Atlantic on uninhabited beaches in northern Namibia. The Kunene constitutes the natural boundary between Namibia and Angola.

The riverbanks are thick with abundant greenery, and are an ideal environment for different species of animals, birds, and insects that are otherwise unknown in Namibia. It is almost perfect croc habitat. Numerous avian and mammalian species are forced to come to the river to drink—some mammals even cross the river in search of new grazing ground—and patient crocs are rewarded with a constant supply of food.

The Epupa Falls are situated in the river's principal trough and spew down approximately 131 feet, creating a dazzling spectacle. Upriver from the falls, natural Jacuzzi-like pools are created, and it is generally assumed that these pools are croc free. They are the only places in the river where it is considered safe to swim.

In April 2005, Mannetjies Coetzer, a successful, thirty-five-year-old businessman from Heidelberg, Namibia, made the fatal mistake of taking what he assumed was going to be a cooling dip in the river. Whether he was in one of the protected pools or in the river proper is not known. The refreshing swim in knee-high water abruptly ended, turning instantly into a futile fight for his life, when a Nile crocodile got ahold of him underwater and immediately pulled him down in typical croc fashion.

Watching from the shore, his brother, Lukas Coetzer a pastor from Nylstroom East, saw an unexpected whirlpool as the croc lashed his tail from side to side like a rudder in the water. The brother jumped in (some would say foolishly) to try to save the victim. His efforts were in vain. In southern Malawi, the low-lying Lower Shire Valley is home to several large game parks that attract many tourists yearly, making substantial monetary contributions to both the local and national economies. The valley is also the home of deadly crocs that kill at least two Malawians every day.

Some Malawian experts blame this on the government's obligations under CITES (Congress of International Trade in Endangered Species). Before signing the treaty, Malawi used to kill about 800 crocodiles annually, but the treaty only allows 200 crocs to be killed in any given year. In spite of international wildlife treaties, some local authorities have taken it upon themselves to employ professional hunters to cull killer crocs.

Ironically, at least where Malawians are concerned, the IUCN Red List categorizes the Nile crocodile as a low risk species of least concern. It may be threatened in some parts of its range, but overall, its population is healthy, and the prognosis for the future of the reptile is excellent.

During one month in 2000, the Malawian Department of Parks and Recreation authorized the killing of 100 crocodiles. Wildlife minister George Ntafu said his ministry suspected witchcraft was responsible for the proliferation of crocodile attacks on people. The practice of witchcraft is alive and well in many parts of rural (and even urban) Africa. Belief in the supernatural is constantly reinforced by shamans, especially among uneducated, superstitious people and tribes that form the majority of rural populations.

Villagers in Nanalide (which is 37 miles south of the country's commercial capital, Blantyre) are terrified because of the increase in croc-human contacts. In January 2005, Maira Semu's husband went fishing as he often did at a local river. He never came back. Some of his remains were found by a search party. Loss of habitat and depleted stocks of wild fish caused by overfishing are blamed for the increased number of attacks.

The Lower Shire River has seen a dramatic increase in human population and a reduction of both croc habitat and suitable prey. This may account for the increased number of attacks on humans. A conservation program, the Zambezi Basin Wetlands Conservation and Resource Utilization Project, is attempting to educate people and conserve croc habitat.

In central Malawi, crocodile farming is a key economic activity. One ranch currently rears around 2,500 crocs. Tail meat and the exporting of hides for shoes and bags (France is the ranch's biggest customer) are the primary yields.

Nile crocs lurk in the densely populated districts of Nsanje and Chikwana where people grow crops and bathe and wash in rivers. In a several-month span in 2001, at least 500 people were attacked. Blind people are especially at risk. During the attacks in 2001, at least three people without sight were killed and another six badly injured. Local officials admit there are probably more attacks resulting in deaths and injuries, but concede that many villagers do not bother reporting them to authorities.

Not all croc attacks in Malawi result in fatalities. One of those victims who lived to tell the tale was an unnamed woman who in May 2000 was attacked in the central lakeshore district of Nkhota Kota, one of Africa's oldest market towns and once a center of a flourishing slave trade. She was captured on a lake beach where she had gone to collect water. (In the previous month, there had been eight attacks on the same lake.) Onlookers came to her rescue and bravely fought with the croc. They managed to rescue the woman, who was in danger of losing a badly mangled arm. But she kept her life.

A sugar company in the district denied responsibility. It used to rear crocodiles for food and export on its land, but when the company was sold to another sugar company, the new owners decided they did not need the reptiles. A spokesman said the former croc owners did not release crocodiles into the lake where the woman was attacked, but conceded that one or two might have strayed into the water.

In December 2002, businessman Mac Bosco Chawinga, forty-three, foolishly went swimming in a lake in the northern Nkhata Bay district, where a crocodile grabbed him. Nkhata Bay is a busy port and market, and a favorite stopping place for travelers.

Bob Mtekama, a senior police officer in the area, said, "Both his arms were inside the full-sized crocodile's jaws, and the beast was dragging him into deeper waters when he decided to fight back."

Chawinga sunk his teeth into the croc's nose, and miraculously, the reptile released him. The badly bitten businessman somehow managed to drag himself to shore where he was found by local fishermen who rushed him to a local hospital. He made a full recovery and kept his arms and his life.

Twenty-six-year-old Kenyan Hillary Amuma also made the right decision when he was attacked by a crocodile on the banks of the River Tana where he had gone to fish. While wading in waist-deep water, he felt something pull on his left thigh. When he instinctively hit back, his hand was bitten. He realized he was in the jaws of a Nile crocodile. Remembering what he had been taught as a child, Amuma jabbed at the croc's eyes with two fingers.

The reptile reacted instinctively and tried to save its eyes, which are perhaps the only vulnerable place on a croc's body. The croc released him and then used its powerful tail to springboard up and out of the water.

The animal leapt over Amuma, hoping to crash down and subdue him with its massive body weight. In anticipation of the kill, the croc's massive, tooth-filled jaws were wide open. When Amuma looked back at the nearby village and saw no one in sight, he knew he had to either fight or die.

The Kenyan somehow managed to keep his composure and viciously poked at the croc's eyes a second time. When the animal backed away, he made his escape. The entire episode took over thirty desperate minutes, in what amounted to a macabre ballet between the hunter and the hunted. Amuma was treated at a local clinic for two weeks for minor wounds and released.

■ ■ Women who fetch water at the river often throw stones first as a precaution, to disturb and frighten any croc that may be lurking beneath the surface. This is where a hunting croc is perhaps the most dangerous. They are concealed and very close. By using their strong, heavy tails, they are more than capable of leaping out of the water, grabbing a victim in a viselike grip, and retreating back into the safety of deeper water, where the victim typically drowns.

The St. Lucia River flows through Kenya into South Africa. It is a broad waterway, and in 2002 was the scene of an oil spill from an Italian cargo ship that threatened the Greater St. Lucia Wetlands Park. The Wetlands is a huge, shallow estuary system, and a World Heritage site on the coast of KwaZulu-Natal. There is a St. Lucia Crocodile Center, and it was there that oil-soaked birds and crocs were cleaned, rehabilitated, and released.

The Wetlands Park, which contains numerous reserves, different ecological zones, and St. Lucia Lake is a very popular tourist destination. The lake boasts a croc population of approximately 1,500 that feeds on a smorgasbord of readily available wildlife. Life for the river crocs is good too. Because of the abundance of food and ample space, which allows them to claim individual territories, they are large and aggressive.

In addition to thousands of tourists, many local people interact with the river in a variety of ways, including bathing, washing clothes, gathering water, and fishing. Most do so without suffering unpleasant consequences.

Neville Elder, seventy-five, was not so fortunate. He went fishing in the St. Lucia River in March of 2005 and never returned. He had been to the river many times before and nothing out of the ordinary had ever happened. KwaZulu-Natal Wildlife officials later killed a crocodile believed responsible for the attack. Drag marks leading to the river indicated Elder was taken by the croc on land, possibly while he slept. It is not uncommon for people to camp overnight by the river, and by and large, it's a relatively safe practice.

Crocs often hunt at night. Elder probably never heard the croc until he was in its jaws, and by then it was too late. His frantic cries for help were unanswered; his fate sealed in a bone-breaking chomp. Divers recovered what was left of him—what the croc didn't eat—floating in the water.

November and December of 1999 saw three fatal attacks. The first was a female staff member of the Crocodile Center who was working with KwaZulu-Natal Wildlife at Lake Bhangazi in the Greater St. Lucia Wetlands Park. She should have known it was very dangerous to fish near the water's edge; or maybe she did know and decided to take a chance, or perhaps she had believed it was safe. By the time she realized her mistake, it was obviously too late. Her body was never found, even after an extensive search was conducted.

A multitude of stars shone like miniature diamonds sprinkled randomly by an unseen hand, high in the African summer night sky on December 8. A pleasing and welcome breeze created a cooling contrast to the brain-numbing heat that had almost overwhelmed park visitors that day.

Tracy Hunt, a twenty-two-year-old female South African tourist, couldn't resist the inviting, slow-moving water of the St. Lucia Estuary/Umfolozi River mouth, and for reasons known only to herself, she decided to go for a nude swim with her boyfriend Claudio Celestino in the middle of the night.

Not a good idea in croc-infested waters!

What was intended to be a romantic rendezvous turned into a date with death, when she unwittingly served herself up as a late-night snack for hungry Nile crocodiles. Celestino said he heard his girlfriend scream in pain before she disappeared under the water. Wildlife officers and policemen recovered the victim's dismembered remains thirty-six hours after the attack.

Two days later a local woman was crossing the Enseleni River. Villagers often cross the Enseleni on foot, since there are no bridges. A huge croc grabbed her and bit her before hauling her underwater, where she drowned. Witnesses later said the croc held her lifeless body in its jaws, but for some reason did not attempt to feed on her remains. Eventually, the corpse was recovered, more or less intact.

■ ■ ■

The Limpopo River arises in the interior of Africa and wends its way from the South African-Zimbabwe border to just south of the port city of Xai-Xai, where it empties its muddy contents into the Indian Ocean. The Limpopo also separates South Africa on its southeast bank from Botswana in the northwest. Zimbabwe is to the north.

Vasco da Gama was the first European to see the river when one of his expeditions anchored off its mouth in 1498. Rudyard Kipling immortalized the river in a short story, entitled "The Elephant's Child." Fourteen million people live in the Limpopo River Basin. Most are poor, and malnutrition and starvation are not uncommon during periodic crop failures or droughts.

On January 11, 1988, a deranged preacher from the Apostolic Faith sect knelt on the banks upriver, closed his eyes, and fervently prayed. He told his followers he had received divine guidance that God had cleared the way for them across the flood-swollen and crocodile-infested river. Twenty-nine sect members believed him and dutifully followed the preacher into the river, where waiting crocs promptly ate them. Three days later the death toll had risen to thirty-six.

During July and August 2004, three people lost their lives to crocs in the Ndera Ward of the Tana River district. In addition to humans, the voracious crocs also devoured seventy-six goats and twelve cows.

■ ■ About 85 percent of all attacks occur between November and April, as this coincides with the breeding and nesting season. Air and water temperatures rise during these months, encouraging more activity within the croc community; water levels also rise, and in the murky water, it's all but impossible to detect lurking crocs.

Clal Crocodile Farms Ltd. conducted surveys and interviews in rural Tanzania from December 10, 1994, through February 14, 1995. The survey's mission was to elucidate data on human deaths from crocodile attacks, and the impact of crocodile populations in provincial areas. The eight-member team interviewed chiefs, villagers, and local administrators by day, and conducted croc surveys at night.

The team covered around 620 miles of swamps, rivers, and lakeshores, including the Lower Rufiji between Mpanga and Utete, Kilombero and Kibasira swamps between Mimba and Ifakara, the southeastern shore of Lake Rukwa, the Ruvu River from Ruvu to the Indian Ocean and parts of the Wami and Pangani rivers. Monster-sized crocodiles of up to 20 feet in length, easily capable of swallowing a human whole, were seen in protected areas of the Rufiji, Lake Rukwa, and the lower Pangani.

Death rates resulting from croc attacks were often underestimated. The village of Mpanga on the upper Kilombero lost eight people, including five children, in 1993. Other villages reported similar fatality rates.

Team members attributed the high death rates to a widely dispersed but dense rural population that lived along rivers and lakes. Another contributing factor was the government, which not only disarmed local people, but also maintained strict and extensive antiwildlife poaching units in every region of the country. Local people feared the antipoaching units as much as they feared the crocs.

Not all killer crocs are slain. On March 8, 2005, three Ugandan wildlife experts accompanied by two rangers captured a 16.6-foot-long reptile near the village of Lugaga on the shores of Lake Victoria, using ropes and nets. They had camped in the bush and mosquito-infested, dank Lugaga swamp for three long, sweaty nights.

The beast weighed nearly 2,000 pounds and was reported to have eaten more than eighty-three people over the past twenty years. It took fifty strong fishermen to remove the gargantuan creature from the water. Once it was caught, the croc's jaws were securely tied shut with ropes before the giant reptile was loaded into the back of a pickup truck and taken away so it could be relocated.

Most of the victims of this croc were fishermen on Lake Victoria, off the shores of the Bugiri district. Other casualties were villagers who'd been collecting water from the lake. Residents of Lugaga make their homes for the most part in mud huts, living off the fish they catch in the lake. Approximately 9,600 people reside in Lugaga.

A local croc expert said it was common knowledge that the crocodile took its victims to a special place where it allowed the bodies to decompose for several days before eating them at its leisure. The villagers called the croc's dining place the "Butcher."

The croc, estimated to be about sixty years old, was relocated to a sanctuary in Buwama, 45 miles from the capital, Kampala. It had to be moved quickly in order to stop local residents from avenging the deaths. Alex Mutamba, manager of a farm called Uganda Crocs Ltd., said the croc would be part of their breeding stock.

Uganda's website, www.newvision.co.ug, declares that "Killing such animals in the name of vermin control is counterproductive. It depletes populations of scarce animal species, denies the animals their rights to live, and leads to economic loss. In any case, when a crocodile kills a human being for a meal, it does not know that it is doing wrong. When crocodiles eat human beings it is a symptom of an underlying environmental problem such as over-fishing and depletion of their prey."

About 100 crocs live in Uganda's portion of the lake, which Kenya and Tanzania also share.

In 2002 the Uganda Wildlife Authority (UWA) sent an armed patrol to cull predatory crocs that killed more than forty people in the preceding seven months. The killer crocs usually lurked in shallow waters, waiting for their victims, before snatching them and dragging them further offshore. Fishermen and women fetching water, who were often preoccupied with their chores, were particularly at risk.

People strolling down to the beach in front of the Petroleum Club, Plage Sportive in Pointe Noire, Republic of Congo, discovered a most unwelcome visitor in late January 2005. A 21-foot-long croc weighing a massive 4,500 pounds had decided the beach was an excellent and convenient place to bask in the sun.

A frantic call was immediately made by club management to the army, who dispatched the monster croc without incident, much to the relief of beachgoers. During the past several months, villagers who lived near Pointe Noire had complained to authorities that some of their neighbors had suddenly gone mysteriously missing.

Was the giant croc the culprit? No human remains were found in the animal's stomach, but experts estimated his age at a minimum of eighty years, and concluded he was too old and too slow to catch his normal prey. He might have been gobbling up villagers because they were easier to capture.

The Nairobi Times reported on January 21, 2000, that Kenyan wildlife wardens had to intercede to deter a mob of prostitutes from pilfering the genitals from the corpse of a croc they had killed in Lake Victoria. Streetwalkers in the town of Mbita tried to remove the reptile's private parts after wildlife officials killed the animal while hunting for a rogue hippo. Apparently, some prostitutes superstitiously believe that croc testicles are a strong love potion.

Working in Kenya was a dream-come-true for eighteen-year-old Amy Nichols. The pretty blonde Briton was in the country in March 2002 as part of her gap year, working on an environmental teaching project organized by Africa and Asia Adventure. Before entering college, many students in the United Kingdom take a year off and enroll in programs that allow them to study abroad. Environmental issues are among the most popular, and travel and relaxation are also important components of the trips. For Amy Nichols, however, her dream trip would quickly morph into the worst nightmare imaginable.

Amy decided to visit scenic Lake Challa with a group of friends on one of her weekends off. She was seeking a little rest and recuperation, a brief respite from the enjoyable but tiring project that had occupied so much of her time and energy in recent months. After pitching their tents and stowing their gear, Amy and her friends were hot and sweaty. The lake waters nearby were irresistible. The staff at a local hotel assured them without hesitation that it was perfectly safe to swim in the lake.

Sometimes it's best to double-check.

By early evening, Amy and two friends were standing in the water. Nesting birds filled the trees, socializing and vocalizing. Suddenly Amy disappeared, dragged under the water's surface by something large and powerful that no one saw or heard.

The Kenyan Wildlife Service claimed the lake was free of crocodiles, but a spokesman from the Nairobi police department contradicted that assertion, stating that, "We have established that Lake Challa is infested with crocodiles."

Divers from the Kenyan navy later recovered what was left of Amy's badly mutilated body. One of her arms was missing and she had suffered serious wounds. The Nile crocodile—or Mamba crocodile, as they are called locally—had obviously chewed on her, inflicting many deep bite and puncture marks. Large chunks of her flesh had been torn from her body, leaving gaping holes.

Increased human contact was blamed for the attacks. Authorities speculated that older crocs slowed by age are mainly responsible, because humans are easier to catch than fish. The Uganda Wildlife Authority is trying to help villagers coexist with the very dangerous predatory reptiles by promoting tourism in the area, and selling croc hides and croc eggs as potential sources of income. Whether croc tourism will be economically viable remains to be seen.

■ ■ Most Nile crocodile attacks can be categorized into four main categories: defense of territory, defense of nest or babies, self-defense, and hunting for food. More attacks occur when warmer waters and air temperatures combine to increase crocodilian activity.

During the dry season when traditional riverine places become too shallow or too crowded, many crocodiles search for deeper water and wind up in places where they are not usually found, thus increasing their chances for contact with humans. All crocodilians are more than capable of traveling reasonable distances on land to search for deeper water, and the food that is invariably to be found in or near it.

The presence of other people doesn't usually deter a croc from attacking its intended victim. Victims have been taken in the midst of noisy groups of men, women, and children who were crossing a river, washing food or clothes, or bathing. Once a croc, gator, or caiman locks onto a target, it is very difficult (if not impossible) to dissuade them from breaking off the attack.

Upon seizing a victim, a croc rarely if ever releases its grip. There are exceptions, of course, and these have been previously noted; however, they are rare. Fighting back in no way guarantees escape. To a hungry croc or gator, a struggling human is just like any other animal battling for its life. Usually the croc wins. The humans that live to tell the tale of fighting off an attacking croc are few and far between. They are the lucky ones.

Throwing rocks, thrusting spears, stabbing with knives, beating with a cudgel or paddle, or using any other weapon at hand typically does not deter a croc. The animal's armor-plated skin protects it. It is akin to bouncing a tennis ball off an elephant's tough hide. A croc's eyes are its only vulnerable spot, and even then, unless the victim is extremely fortunate, a poke or jab will usually miss the intended target and instead land on osteoderm-protected hide.

Attacks on boats and canoes result when the croc sees the silhouette or the shape of the craft, not its occupants. In many cases the croc will attack the boat, allowing the human occupants to escape. Why an individual would leave the relative safety of a boat or canoe to jump into croc-infested waters is another matter entirely.

The Pangani River emerges from the highlands of Tanzania and passes through the Korogwe District, close to its termination in the Indian Ocean at Pangani. According to the Korogwe Department of Natural Resources (which documents human fatalities due to crocodile attacks), crocodiles have been responsible for fifty-one deaths in this district. These deaths took place in the fifty-two months between January 1990 and April 1994, and of these, eighteen fatalities occurred during the first four months of 1994.

The following chart depicts the deaths caused by crocodiles, and deaths of the crocodiles, from 1990 to 1994 in the Korogwe District. Although the data is somewhat dated, by extrapolation the chart is a reasonable facsimile of the collective fates of humans and crocodiles who are forced to coexist in close proximity in these parts of Africa.

Date	Human Deaths	Crocodile Deaths
1990	5	10
1991	9	5
1992	8	8
1993	11	10
1994 (January to April only)	18	16
TOTAL	51	49

The district consists of roughly twenty villages, with a population of 217,810 (according to the 1988 census). The crocodile population is thought to number 600. In other words, one croc for every 361 people—a ratio that should keep both people and crocs happy.

It is believed that crocodile attacks on people have increased primarily due to overfishing, which reduces the croc's food supply, and also, the fact that food waste products are being disposed of in the river. Such disposal would naturally attract crocs and bring them into even closer contact with humans.

Additionally, many traditional beliefs concerning crocodiles have been corrupted. For example, it is thought by numerous indigenous people that crocodiles only attack men and women, not boys. Ergo, boys can swim in croc-infested waters with impunity.

After an attack occurs, witch doctors will often "consult" with crocodiles in order to determine which croc is responsible. The offender is then slain.

In impoverished, underdeveloped third-world countries, infrastructures are either nonexistent or barely adequate at best. By Western standards, even basic medical care is appallingly lacking. This no doubt contributes substantially to the annual death toll, when people who have been severely maimed by marauding crocs subsequently die due to inadequate medical care for the trauma and ensuing infections. Attacks often occur in remote areas that are miles (and hours) away from the nearest clinic or hospital. Many victims die en route.

In the event a victim reaches an adequate medical facility, the recovery period can be prolonged, painful, and expensive. The sharp, pointed teeth of the crocodile invariably inject pathogenic bacteria deep into the victim's flesh and muscle tissue. The tremendous force with which a crocodile closes its jaws and slices through the victim's flesh often results in tissue necrosis, which in turn creates extremely advantageous circumstances for anaerobic bacterial infections—many of which are resistant to antibiotics. In such cases, amputations are sometimes necessary to save the patient's life.

It should also be noted that the vast majority of people do not get bitten on the fingers. Because a croc's jaws are so strong and wide, it prefers to clamp down on arms, legs, buttocks, or torsos, which obviously present bigger targets. The loss of a finger is minimal compared to losing an arm or leg. The amputee is in many instances unable to work and contribute to the general well-being of his family or village, thus creating additional burdens and hardships for an already impoverished community.

Some of these countries are ruled by despots with iron fists; and some nations are plagued by religious or tribal-based civil wars that rage unresolved for decades. These wars invariably create fractious societies, making those least able to fend for themselves even more vulnerable. Corruption is not unknown, and many heads of state have clan loyalties that create a more divisive society. The annual death toll due to crocodile attacks is in many instances simply regarded as a fact of life by local people, who are forced to deal with the reptiles on a daily basis.

By and large, the general rural public is at the mercy of these prehistoric predators, who strike on their own terms in a place and time of their own choosing.

CROCODILES IN THE SAHARA

Nile crocodiles are eking out a living in the Sahara desert. A smallish (approximately 328 square feet) pond located 125 miles from the nearest river in southern Mauritania is home to a modest population of crocs. First discovered in the late 1990s, the pond contains large numbers of microorganisms which encourage the presence of weeds, which in turn supports the fish the crocodiles feed on. Local people believe that killing the crocodiles would cause the pond to dry up. The crocs never attack domestic animals such as goats and cattle—or at least, they haven't yet—which drink from the pond.

Other isolated croc colonies (some numbering as many as thirty to forty animals) have been found in Mauritania, living in caves, burrows, and under rocks. The reptiles have successfully adapted to the changing environment. Eight to ten thousand years ago, northern Africa was made up of grasslands, and a lush savannah; now, it is hot and arid.

The desert crocodiles reside in two types of wetlands: lowland wetlands, and a category of wetland known as a *guelta*. A guelta is created when rain or underground springs cause a pool of water to be formed in a basin of a rocky plateau. Lowland wetlands in Mauritania are formed when rainwater accumulates in clay-lined depressions in otherwise dryland conditions.

When the water dries up, the crocodiles *estivate*, spending the summer in a state of inactivity similar to hibernation, which some crocodilian species (including the American alligator) regularly employ as a survival strategy in the colder winter months. Eating and movement are kept to a minimum to conserve energy and retain body fat. Desert-dwelling crocs are much smaller than other Nile crocodiles that reside in lush habitat that has a more abundant food supply.

In spite of these harsh, far-from-ideal conditions, these crocodiles are more fortunate than others because the local inhabitants imbue them with a mythological esteem. The crocs are not feared, and people routinely swim and wade with them. Amazingly, there have been no reports of attacks. The crocodiles are inexorably tied to the life-sustaining water. The common, widely shared belief is that if the crocs go, the water supply will dry up.

These Sahara-dwelling crocs are the direct descendants of another crocodilian whose fossilized remains were found in Gadoufaoua, Niger, during paleontological expeditions from 1997 to 2000. *Sarcosuchus imperator*, the flesh-eating emperor, lived 100 million years ago during the Middle Cretaceous Period, in which dinosaurs became extinct and early mammals and flowering plants developed. The beast weighed as much as 17,500 pounds, grew up to 40 feet long, and had 6-foot-long jaws that contained more than 100 bone-crushing, flesh-tearing teeth.

The Nile crocodile has physically and spiritually dominated its habitat for thousands of years. From the time of the pharaohs to the present day, its demeanor inspires fear, awe, and respect. It is one of the three largest crocodiles in the world, and like the American alligator, reigns supreme in its environment.

Although they may only number in the hundreds, the Nile crocodiles of the Sahara are living examples of the resiliency and adaptability of this species.

The Moremi Game Reserve in Botswana covers approximately 1,880 square miles at the eastern section of the game-rich Okavango Delta. The Moremi has been described as one of the most beautiful wildlife reserves in Africa. Leopard, hyena, baboon, cheetah, hippo, countless species of birds, the extremely endangered wild dog, jackal, and several species of large and small antelope proliferate.

Both black and white rhinos were found in the reserve in the past, but have since been relocated to the protection of a sanctuary to protect them from poachers who kill them for their horns. The horns, made of keratin, are regarded in certain parts of the Far East by traditional herbalists as a panacea for a variety of physical ailments. They are also widely used as an aphrodisiac.

Rivers and lagoons bifurcate and inundate the reserve, providing excellent year-round habitat for a great number of different avian, mammalian, and reptilian species in both the dry and wet seasons. The reserve is governed by the Department of Wildlife and National Parks. There are several, slightly more primitive public campgrounds in addition to the more luxury-oriented sites operated by the reserve. By all accounts, it's an idyllic place.

However, the Edenesque nature of Moremi was suddenly shattered when the reserve experienced its first two recorded attacks by Nile crocodiles in many years. In August 2000, an unidentified male visitor was violently assaulted in the relative comfort and security of his tent. The reserve and its campgrounds are a very successful tourist attraction, popular with people from all over the globe who come in great and consistent numbers to view and photograph wild game.

Organized half-day and full-day safaris, accompanied by an armed guard, take visitors in open-top, four-wheel-drive vehicles to the animals. In this particular instance, the animals—or to be specific, *the* animal—came to the visitor.

It was a most unwelcome guest, and certainly not one the man was expecting. Details are somewhat sketchy, but it's more than likely the attack occurred in the dead of night when the victim was sound asleep. Presumably he was alone in his tent at the time, a not particularly unusual occurrence. The reserve does an admirable job of satisfying the needs of a variety of visitors, who have widely varying economic situations. Some are very wealthy; some are not. Some come in groups or with partners; some do not.

Nile crocs and other crocodilian species often prefer to stalk their prey after the sun has disappeared and the moon has risen.

The croc would have absorbed plenty of energy during the day from the sun, and the heat would not only increase the animal's appetite, but also allow it to digest its meal more easily.

A sleeping man, whether he is in a tent or in the open, is a very easy meal.

The victim did not survive the attack. Much to the chagrin of reserve officials, the incident took place in the same camp where an American boy was recently dragged from his tent and eaten alive by a pack of hyenas.

Also attacked in his tent was a safari company driver who managed to grab hold of a steel pole and fight back, thereby saving his life. A Botswana Defense Force helicopter airlifted the victim to a hospital in Maun, where he recovered from his wounds.

Could these attacks have been prevented? Any prudent person would be aware of the fact that although the chances of being attacked while in a camp are relatively rare, incidents do happen. Once entering a game preserve, no matter where it happens to be in the world, man is no longer at the top of the food chain. There are many animals that would gladly eat a human, because they are so easy to catch and kill.

■ ■ Hippos won't eat people, but they do kill them fairly regularly. Venomous snakes are responsible for almost countless numbers of human deaths in Africa, but they don't consume humans either. It is the big constrictors that swallow men whole.

It is likely that many people, including those who visit game parks, are either misinformed or ignorant of crocodilian habits. They are probably lacking a general knowledge of what the reptile is capable of, and what it isn't.

Although a Nile croc's natural habitat is water, they also hunt on land, as do other species of crocodilians. There have been documented instances of Nile crocodiles driving hungry lionesses away from a freshly killed carcass hundreds of yards from the nearest water. Crocs appear to be lumbering and clumsy when out of their natural element, and to an extent, this is true. However, they are quite mobile on terra firma. Most crocodilians can scamper for short distances at speeds of around 20 miles per hour. More to the point, they can move relatively quietly. Any animal that earns its living by stalking knows the value of being deathly quiet. Patience and stealth are virtues that have favorably served hungry crocs for millions of years.

Africa at night, especially in the middle of nowhere—which is where most game reserves are situated—tends to be a very noisy place. Chirps, squawks, croaks, grunts, groans, screeches, and roars create a concert of what seems to the uneducated ear a symphony of absolute chaos. Diurnal animals seek shelter and safety, while nocturnal hunters wake, yawn, and leave their lairs. It is the beginning of the night shift.

Utilizing the cover of darkness, it is entirely possible a crocodile could slip in under the radar, so to speak, and make its way undetected to a tent. Moonless African nights are coal-black. It is perfect cover for a black-and-dark-olive-colored Nile croc. A low-to-the-ground, 1,000-pound animal becomes invisible, for all intents and purposes.

A person exhausted from an exhilarating day spent animal watching under Africa's strength-sapping, scorchingly hot sun and heat would have no difficulty succumbing to a deep and well-deserved sleep. However, a tent can also give its occupant a false sense of security and well-being. Canvas or nylon walls are at best protection against rain and sun, and perhaps annoying insects. They will not deter any large mammalian or reptilian animal intent on getting a meal.

Because it hugs the ground, a croc, no matter how large, would have little difficulty in exploiting any gaps or spaces where doors are not completely closed. The croc's excellent sense of smell would allow it to locate the precise position of a sleeping human form with no difficulty whatsoever.

Once inside the limited-space tent, where there is only room for a normal-sized person to stand, and perhaps a cot, folding chair, and maybe a small table, the occupant would be unable to flee. Disoriented and terrified at such a rude awakening, the victim would have little chance of survival once in the grip of a croc's jaws.

The quarry would instantly go into shock from the force of the initial bite, and the remainder of the attack sequence would be academic. The loss or severe mangling of an arm or leg and the accompanying loss of blood would render the human prey unconscious within seconds, or minutes at most. If the croc decided not to eat the victim right away, it could easily drag it back into the safety of a nearby body of water—in this case, a river—again concealing its movements within the inky black, cacophonous African night.

Visitors to game parks in Africa, or any other place in the world, should be aware that danger and potential death lurks where it is least expected. Every now and then death pays an unexpected visit, walking on clawed tiptoes, moving silently as a shadow.

As elephant habitat continues to shrink, rampaging elephants routinely destroy crops and trample villagers to death while in search of food. Twelve people, mostly villagers trying to protect their harvests, were charged or trampled by the giant herbivores in Zimbabwe in 2005. Hippos and exceedingly dangerous, curved-horned buffalo were responsible for the deaths of two people. Crocodiles ate twelve people (adults and children), putting them on top of a macabre list of killer animals.

One person crocs in Zimbabwe didn't eat was Letikuku Sidumbu, forty-two, who was attacked while attempting to cross the rain-swollen Mubvinzi River in the Goromonzi district, about twenty-five miles east of Harare. Sidumbu was on an early-morning hunting junket, accompanied by his uncle and several dogs.

The croc clamped its jaws on his right arm as he implored his uncle to clobber the croc with an ax. The hunting dogs' yowls alerted nearby villagers, who ran to the victim's rescue and attempted to pull him free. The ensuing tug-of-war that saw the croc on one end, Sidumbu in the middle, and the villagers on the other end eventually resulted in the victim's escape. In addition to puncture wounds on his arm, he also suffered a broken leg and numerous chest and stomach injuries.

▨ ▪ Far to the north, in the ancient land which deified the Nile crocodile thousands of years ago, fishermen are forced to compete with the reptiles for their livelihoods. There are thirty-two species of fish found in Lake Nasser, Egypt. Approximately 5,000 fishermen regularly ply the lake, catching around 80,000 tons of fish per year.

Lake Nasser is an artificial lake. The Aswan High Dam was built in the 1960s. Construction began in 1964 by order of President Gamal Abdul Nasser. The dam is over 11,000 feet long, approximately 3,200 feet thick at its base, and 364 feet high. It contains around eighteen times the amount of material used in the Great Pyramid of Cheops.

The High Dam was built around three miles downriver from the Low Dam, and together these dams provide irrigation and electricity for all of Egypt. The world's largest man-made reservoir, Lake Nasser, was created at the same time. The High Dam established 30 percent more cultivatable land in Egypt and raised the water table for the Sahara as far away as Algeria.

Lake Nasser is a boon for its resident crocs and the excited tourists who regularly flock to see them basking or swimming. These saurian monsters of the Nile continue to fascinate people and inspire awe and fear, and perhaps begrudging respect. Water birds use the lake as a refuge, and this too attracts camera-clicking tourists and hungry crocs that are always on the lookout for an easy-to-catch meal. Nile crocodiles annually eat around 30 percent of the fish found in the lake.

In 2003 a croc ate a fisherman.

This did not signal an increase of attacks on fishermen and was regarded as something of an aberration. A well-fed Nile crocodile will not necessarily prefer to attack a human as opposed to other prey items.

All crocodilians are opportunistic hunters. A 2,000-pound animal, no matter how efficiently it utilizes its fuel or source of energy, nevertheless requires a substantial amount of food to not only sustain its life but also to maintain its ability to effectively hunt, mate, and defend its territory.

With the activation of an Egyptian environmental protection edict in 1983 that prohibits the hunting or killing of Nile crocs (including killer crocs) among other species, like the Nile turtle, croc numbers have spiraled in the lake. Lake Nasser, all 2,394 square miles of it, falls under this law, which legislates the safeguarding of 7 percent of the total Egyptian state for the protection of crocs and other species.

Egyptian law number 102, which addresses the protection of reservoirs, was proclaimed to prohibit actions such as poaching for croc skins and water pollution that might lead to a decrease of crocodile populations. Ten years ago Egypt signed an international agreement (CITES) that protected rare species, including the Nile crocodile.

The environmental protection law of 1983 and the international agreement effectively help and protect Egypt's wildlife. Experts agree that healthy numbers of Nile crocs in Lake Nasser protect other species at the same time. They help the environment by eating large numbers of barbel catfish, which are predators themselves. Barbels eat other fish which make up the diet of more than forty species of birds. If birds leave an area because there are no edible fish, the amount of guano they produce that normally provides nutrients for the fish declines, and the food chain is disrupted.

Fishermen routinely catch in their nets groups of small Nile crocs, and presumably they are killed on the spot. Hunting the crocs on a large scale is not only banned but also an environmentally unsound practice.

In 1996 it was verified by independent witnesses that street vendors in Luxor and the bazaar offered around twenty-five live juvenile crocs for sale, crocs that came from Lake Nasser. Stuffed specimens were also for sale in the Valley of the Kings in Luxor.

However, the economic and physical damage, such as torn or ruined nets, done to Lake Nasser's fishermen pales in comparison to the havoc wreaked on a general population by what was arguably the most famous (or infamous) killer croc in Africa: Gustave.

Burundi, once known as Urundi, was controlled by Germany from 1884, and by Belgium from 1919, until gaining its independence in 1962. The country's recent history is replete with bloody battles between the Hutu and Tutsi, which resulted in a genocide that many people compared in ferocity and numbers of people killed to the horrors in neighboring Rwanda. Less than 50 percent of Burundi's children attend school, HIV/AIDS is out of control, and basic foods and medicines are in short supply.

The country has a high population density (contraception is practiced very little and is socially frowned upon, at least by males), and extremely limited natural resources. The vast majority of Burundi's citizens are economically suppressed and engage in subsistence agricultural farming. Around 8 million impoverished people live in Burundi. The major religions are Christianity, Catholicism, and traditional beliefs.

Burundi is located in Eastern Africa and is bordered on the north by Rwanda, on the west by Zaire, and on the south and east by Tanzania. Burundi's rivers flow into two basins of two major rivers, the Zaire and the Nile. The most important river flowing into the Zaire basin is the Rusizi, which has its source in Lake Kivu and forms the border between Zaire and Burundi.

The country was one of the few nations in Africa not to have had a national park established during the colonial era. Forestland was established as official reserves by Belgian colonial authorities in 1933. As of 1980 there was no legislation that addressed the issue of protected areas.

The National Institute for the Environment and the Conservation of Nature (INECN) is accountable for the development and administration of all Burundi's national parks and nature reserves.

Other responsibilities include the organization of scientific studies, the encouraging of animal and tree species diversification, ensuring the maximum use and economic potential of all tourist sites in coordination with the National Office of Tourism, the training of nature conservation technicians, and the making of proposals to the president of the Republic for new sites to be protected as parks or reserves.

Probably the most accessible of Burundi's national parks is the Rusizi National Park. It is a wetland environment and provides excellent habitat for hippos, statungas (aquatic antelopes), a wide variety of birds and fish, and bus-size killer crocs.

Gustave snatched people with impunity from the banks of the muddy Rusizi River for decades. His kill total was reputed to be 300 men, women, and children, plus an adult hippo. The latter was very unique. Hippos and crocodiles share the same habitat and have a begrudging respect for each other. They rarely come into physical contact. Gustave's victims were either in the water or on the banks, where malarial mosquitoes flit and buzz with a fierceness known to few other places in Africa.

The rampaging reptile was named by Patrice Faye, a French environmentalist who has worked in Burundi for more than twenty years. He said the name has no particular significance.

Gustave's technique warranted the begrudging admiration of local experts. The croc, reported to be upwards of 30 feet long but in reality closer to 20, apparently used his powerful tail to splash fishermen as they stood in the shallow draft boats and canoes they typically use when fishing. If they were unfortunate enough to fall into the water, Gustave ate them. They were fishing for fish; Gustave was fishing for them.

Although the hunting technique sounds somewhat apocryphal, crocodiles and all crocodilians do have the ability to learn and to make certain associations. It is entirely possible that Gustave eventually learned that splashing men standing in canoes or boats equated into a tasty, readily served meal.

He also grabbed villagers from the riverbanks or the northeastern shores of Lake Tanganyika as they washed, bathed, or gathered water. Gustave was as crafty as he was large, and he eluded capture for years. His prodigious appetite for all human beings and his ability to successfully elude capture attracted worldwide media attention. He became a legend in his own time. Articles appeared in major newspapers, and film crews waited anxiously as various experts from different countries set baited traps in futile efforts to catch the wily beast.

Eventually Gustave became a victim of his own appetite and was finally captured in a well-baited trap. No doubt the villagers sighed collectively in relief when the monster croc was finally removed.

There will always be Gustaves in Africa's lakes and rivers. It is only a matter of time before another killer croc emerges into the public eye. How many people will be eaten is a matter of conjecture. There are certainly no shortages of hungry, opportunistic crocodiles or people ready to be fed upon.

Considering the hunting tools crocodiles have at their disposal, this is not surprising.

As juvenile crocodiles and all crocodilians grow and mature, the size of their eyes do not increase. Like their walnut-size brain, their eyes will remain the same size and have the same properties throughout the animal's life. Crocodilians have three eyelids per eye. One set protects the eyes when the animal is fighting for territory, a mate, or catching prey, and another pair is used like windshield wipers to clear the eyes. Their semitransparent third eyelids are called "nictitating membranes," and are the croc equivalent of Speedo goggles. They lie just beneath the outer eyelids and automatically close to protect the eyes when underwater. The nictitating membranes prevent the eyes from focusing when submerged.

Croc and gator eyes have a vertical pupil that can open wider at night to allow more light to enter than would be possible in a round pupil. A reflective layer called the *tapetum lucidum* lies beneath the retina. The cells of the tapetum contain guanin crystals that form a mirrorlike layer, which reflects most of the incoming light through the light-receptor cells of the eye. These crystals produce the characteristic red-eye shine when hit by light at night. A green or yellow shine indicates a frog or water spider.

Croc eyesight is excellent at night when their large pupil dilates. This allows them more hunting opportunities. During the day the vertical pupil constricts. The pupil will remain vertical to the horizon no matter how or in what direction the crocodile, alligator, caiman, or gharial slants its head. It functions exactly like the artificial horizon indicator in airplanes or helicopters.

Objects that are both close and far away can be distinctly seen by crocs and gators (and also caiman and gharials), but they are hampered by limited depth perception. Their vision is binocular (focusing both eyes on an object at the same time), although it's incomplete because the eyes are positioned on opposite sides of their heads.

Croc ears (and the ears of all crocodilians) are located behind the eyes and are equipped with two watertight folds that cover the ears when the animal submerges. Sound is a fundamental component to many predators, especially those who move with ease between air and water.

The definitive response to all sound, whether perceived in air or water, is driven by the activation of sensory hair cells in the inner ear, and animals that are responsive to airborne sounds convert the sensory signals in the brain stem region of the brain. Crocs don't depend on hearing sound received by their ears when they're submerged. Jawbones are extremely receptive to vibrations. The sounds they capture are mainly in tones of low and subsonic frequency.

All crocodilians are acutely aware of just about anything and anyone that moves around in their environment, and that includes people who come to the riverbanks in Africa to fetch water, bathe, and wash. It also includes people who swim and splash in lakes, rivers, ponds, and canals in Florida—and of course, just about everywhere else in the world where there are crocodilians.

And if for any reason a croc can't see or hear its intended victim, it can always smell it. All crocodilian nostrils are external, positioned on a pad of skin at the end of the snout. Flaps of skin preclude water from invading the air tubes that lead to the rear of the throat and the internal nostrils.

A crocodilian lurking in the weeds. Alligators and crocodiles are often mistaken for logs or rocks in the water.

An African slender-snout feeding.

©Michael Garlock

Gators watching.

A false gharial wolfs down a meal.

©Michael Garlock

A croc displays
its jumping
ability.

An American crocodile at rest.

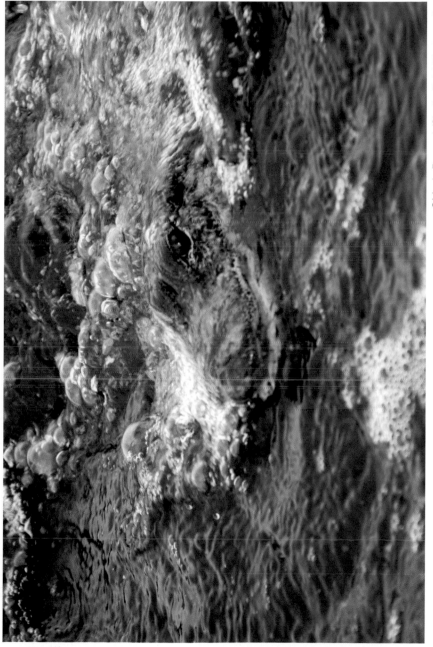

An alligator rolls the water in attack mode.

Crocodilians anxiously awaiting their next meal.

Chemical receptors in a croc's mouth and jaw recognize even the faintest chemical changes in the water, enabling it to taste potential food sources that are great distances away. Crocs can smell carrion for miles, and it is not uncommon to see dozens of them feeding on a large carcass.

Because they cannot chew, crocs often display a degree of cooperation when feeding. One croc will hold a large piece of meat stationary in its jaws while another animal grabs a section and spins. The force is enough to tear muscles and sinews into swallowable chunks. Dismemberment by crocodile is quick and efficient.

There are hundreds of bumpy receptors on the animal's body that can detect a thirsty animal taking a drink, a splashing fisherman reeling in his catch, or a villager wading in knee-deep water washing clothes or dining utensils. The receptors have nerve endings that lead directly to the large trigeminal nerve in the skull that stimulates the skin and facial muscles. After the trigeminal nerve fires, it sends a message to the croc's brain.

Called ISOs (integumentary sense organs), they allow the croc (and all crocodilians) to orient its head toward pressure changes in the water. An alligator only has ISOs on its head. Crocodiles and caimans have them on every scale on their bodies, making them extremely sensitive.

The faintest vibration in the water is sure to arouse a croc's curiosity and trigger an investigation, with results that are usually fatal. When it is stimulated, any crocodilian is immediately on automatic pilot. It doesn't have to think because everything has been preprogrammed into its DNA. Crocodilians are hard-wired hunters and ambushers.

It is akin to dangling a length of string in front of a kitten. The kitten reacts almost instantly in ways that most of us find pleasing, endearing, and amusing. A reacting crocodile or alligator elicits responses that are quite different.

When stalking an intended victim, a Nile crocodile can hold its breath underwater for an hour. This is about the average for all crocodilians. They are patient, cautious hunters, and often watch and wait for just the right opportunity to launch an attack. When submerged they walk on the tips of their claws to avoid disturbing the silt on the bottom and betraying their presence. They are almost impossible to see when underwater, especially when the water is cloudy or murky (which it almost always is).

When surfaced their coloration blends in nearly perfectly with the riverine or lakeside foliage and underbrush.

Once it has selected a victim, the croc slowly closes in for the kill, knowing that any sudden or unexpected movement will disturb the water and betray its presence. The tail moves back and forth in a slow essing motion. Legs are tucked against the sides of the animal, creating a more streamlined shape and reducing drag. Water flows evenly over the osteoderm-lined back, increasing stability.

Lying either below the surface of the water or just above it, with only its eyes and nostrils visible, the croc, gator, or caiman, thanks to its binocular vision, can accurately estimate the distance between itself and its intended victim. Like a stalking submarine, the animal surfaces to have a good look around before it submerges for the last time. The attack sequence begins, and the attacker is virtually invisible. Any crocodilian can perform this maneuver effortlessly and at will.

Once the croc decides it is within the killing zone, it uses its powerful tail to launch itself out of the water in an unexpected explosion of energy. Its huge jaws are wide open. Cone-shaped, sharply pointed teeth are ready to snag and grab. In the event the intended prey makes a sudden, unexpected movement to avoid its gaping jaws, the croc can immediately compensate by swinging its head around in a 60-degree arc in either direction.

An attacking croc doesn't have to grab hold with all of its teeth; a dozen are usually enough to secure its prey. If the croc misses (which they often do), the croc's jaws and head, made almost entirely of granite-hard bone, can deliver a sledgehammer blow capable of instantly stunning and immobilizing a victim.

Once it has a firm grip on its human, avian, or animal prey, a croc will crash back down into the water, hoping to land on top of its victim. Even if the bite is not fatal, the sheer weight of the falling 2,000-pound croc is more than enough to render the quarry unconscious.

Violently flinging the quarry is another successful tactic used for millions of years by crocodilians. Ideally, the prey's neck will be broken, rendering it helpless and making further resistance impossible. At the very least, the victim will be paralyzed and rendered insensate. Cartilage, muscles, and sinews become disconnected and detached, making it easier and more energy-efficient for the croc to dismember the prey.

Digging its heels into the river or lake bottom, an adult croc with a very low center of gravity is capable of pulling backward with the immutable force and power of a John Deere tractor. If it is facing away from the shore, a couple of tail swishes will quickly propel the animal and its victim into deeper water, where the quarry quickly drowns. Carcasses are then stashed under or between rocks or logs to allow them to "ripen," and to facilitate the croc's digestive process.

NILE CROCODILES IN MADAGASCAR

Nile crocodiles are not confined to the African continent. Madagascar, land of bug-eyed, matriarchal-societied lemurs and giant, sticky-tongued chameleons, also has a sizeable croc population that devours people on a regular basis. From 1990 to 1995, the number of fatalities was almost half the number of reported attacks, as the following chart illustrates.

Year	Deaths	Reported Attacks
1990	14	27
1991	7	18
1992	11	22
1993	5	16
1994	8	23
1995	12	34

The majority of attacks occurred mainly from November through March, between 4:00 and 6:00 P.M., when women were collecting water and people were coming back from the fields. Many victims were grabbed by a hand or foot while washing, crossing a river, or collecting water.

The villages of Besalampy were under virtual siege from the marauding reptiles that attacked people, livestock, and crops. The crocs could be found in great numbers in pools of water, swamps, and rice fields.

Eleven deaths were attributed to crocs in December 1994 in the vicinity of the Manimbozo and Maratony rivers. Two victims disappeared completely. No traces of them were ever found. Hunting Nile crocodiles in Madagascar is prohibited.

Like many other animals, crocs have made Madagascar-specific adaptations, and at an undisclosed location two hours distant from an international airport, a healthy population was discovered living in and around underground caves. The area is a limestone karst massif, which comprises around 63 miles of underground river systems.

The caves open to the outside via water holes, which in turn are the openings of the underground rivers. The crocs eat fish found in the rivers. They also consume a cow every now and then, easily catching the dim-witted ruminants as they graze in nearby villages. Because the underground environment is not warm enough for breeding, crocs build their nest sites on peat that forms a cover over the nearby mangrove swamps.

Croc predation on humans in Madagascar is attributed to virtually the same reasons as those found in many parts of mainland Africa. People are attacked primarily while washing, bathing, gathering water, or fishing near water.

There are two other species of crocodilians that inhabit Africa, specifically West Africa. The African slender-snout (*Crocodylus cataphractus*) inhabits Angola, Benin, Burkina Faso, Cameroon, Central African Republic, Chad, Ivory Coast, Democratic Republic of Congo, Equatorial Guinea, Gabon, Gambia, Ghana, Guinea, Guinea-Bissau, Liberia, Mali, Mauritania, Nigeria, Senegal, Sierra Leone, Tanzania, United Republic of Togo, and Zambia. Because of its long, narrow snout, it is also known as the African gavial, or gharial.

This highly aquatic species maxes out at around 14 feet and is found primarily in riverine habitat characterized by dense vegetation cover. They can also be found in large lakes. Although it is widely dispersed, the estimated wild population of this secretive creature is unknown. Various reports suggest there could be as many as 50,000 individuals. In many areas across its distribution, the local population is believed to be depleted primarily due to overhunting. Regulated hunting is allowed in Chad, Sierra Leone, Togo, Cameroon, and the Democratic Republic of Congo. Major threats are habitat destruction and subsistence hunting. The IUCN classifies this species as "Possibly Endangered or Vulnerable." A definite classification is not possible due to deficient data.

The largest remaining population of slender-snouts appears to be in the Ogooue River in Gabon. In Liberia, the species is somewhat depleted, and in Chad and Angola, it is severely depleted. It is possible that the slender-snout no longer exists in Nigeria, Zambia, Senegal, Gambia, and Guinea-Bissau. Inadequately implemented safeguards exist in many countries where it is found. No ranching or farming of this species has ever been undertaken.

The average-sized slender-snout eats primarily fish and small aquatic invertebrates. Larger animals may feed opportunistically on larger prey if and when it becomes available. Although attacks on people do occur, documentation is extremely difficult if not impossible to verify.

The second species of African crocodilian is the West African dwarf crocodile (*Osteolaemus tetraspis*), also known as the broad-snouted crocodile, African caiman, and bony crocodile. *Osteolaemus* means "bony throat," and is derived from the Greek *osteon*, meaning "bone," plus *laimus*, Greek for "throat." This refers to the extensive osteoderms on the neck and belly scales. It also has a knob on its snout.

This species range extends through Angola, Benin, Burkina Faso, Cameroon, Central African Republic, Congo, Ivory Coast, Democratic Republic of Congo, Equatorial Guinea, Gabon, Gambia, Ghana, Guinea, Guinea-Bissau, Liberia, Mali, Nigeria, Senegal, Sierra Leone, and Togo.

Survey data on this species is extremely poor. The estimated wild population is between 25,000 and 100,000. Although it is heavily exploited in some areas, its wide distribution warrants an IUCN Red List rating of "Vulnerable."

Populations in Gambia on the northern edge of the species distribution and in Liberia are described as critically dissipated. The Ivory Coast, Lake Volta in Ghana, the Niger and Benue rivers in Nigeria, the Ogooue River in Gabon, the Congo and the Congo/Zaire and Ubangi rivers in the Democratic Republic of Congo, the Cabinda province in Angola, Mali, and Senegal are all believed to have major populations.

Principal threats to the dwarf crocodile are habitat destruction in the form of deforestation and wetland alteration, and uncontrolled hunting. The dwarf croc is extensively utilized for meat for local consumption. In Cameroon and Congo, thousands are sold yearly in provincial markets. In South Africa at local shops, body meat costs approximately 5 U.S. dollars for 2.2 pounds (one kilogram), $4.20 for ribs, and $7.50 for steaks.

Some skins are used for local production of substandard-quality leather products, sold principally in Asia. Many skins are illegally exported to countries within Africa. Commercial hunting has not been a problem, and there has been little incentive for management programs based on sustainable use.

This species is one of the more diminutive crocodilians. The maximum recorded length is 6.3 feet (1.9 meters). The average length of males and females is somewhat shorter. Its stubby, blunt snout resembles the snout of a caiman. The dwarf croc eats fish, frogs, lizards, crustaceans, and possibly other terrestrial prey.

It prefers to live in slow-moving, calm bodies of water such as swamps and swamp forests, and it can survive in isolated pools in savannah habitat. In forested areas it hunts at night, especially after heavy rains. Hatchlings are adept climbers, suggesting that young dwarf crocodiles seek safety from predators in relatively easy-to-reach branches of lower trees.

CROC CONSERVATION

Crocodile conservation in Africa can take many forms. Political will (or lack thereof), pressure from internal or external forces, and a lack of funding and other necessary resources are elements that enter into the equation. Although it is an iconic symbol, the Nile croc is regarded as a legitimate threat to human life in many areas in which it is found.

Livestock such as cattle and goats, a precious resource in many semi-indigent communities, is also endangered by this large reptile. Extirpation of the Nile croc is widespread in numerous parts of Africa. Control by local authorities is often lax at best, nonexistent at worst.

Many indigenous peoples have a laissez-faire attitude toward crocodiles that borders on the fatalistic. Although people obviously take precautions when venturing near or into croc-infested waters, this innate relaxed perspective no doubt results in many unnecessary deaths and injuries.

When croc numbers become overly large in a given area, and start to dramatically reduce local human populations in horrific fashion, local authorities are more or less forced to act, sometimes in concert with croc experts.

The thriving black market trade in illegal crocodile skins and meat is an integral and vital part of many regional economies. Local and governmental officials throughout Africa are often either unscrupulous or indifferent. Moreover, well-intentioned game wardens or park rangers and quasi-military antipoaching units are frequently underpaid, outgunned, and overmatched by well-organized gangs who are willing to go to great lengths in order to circumvent existing laws and regulations.

Nevertheless, in spite of instances of corruption, lack of funding, political will, and apathy on many different levels, countries make good-faith efforts to protect what is increasingly becoming a valuable natural resource.

Tourists—and the highly valued and sought-after hard currency they bring and freely spend—are being courted by many nations that have sizeable crocodile populations. They realize that ecotourism not only adds considerable income to state coffers, but portions of the tourist proceeds can also be used to protect valuable assets. People have demonstrated with their credit cards, checkbooks, and hard cash that they will pay to see crocs, preferably in their natural habitat.

The Nile crocodile has slowly edged its way up the popularity ladder once dominated by the big cats (usually defined as lions, cheetahs, and leopards), elephants, and hyenas. Increased exposure through worldwide print media and television has made thousands of people aware of how fascinating these giant, prehistoric reptiles are when seen in the wild.

Not all crocs live in inaccessible, malaria-ridden swamps or impenetrable wetland forests where only the very hardy (or foolhardy) venture. A great many reside in habitats shared by other, exceedingly popular-with-tourists animals, such as hippos, ungulates (a hoofed, typically herbivorous quadruped mammal) elephants, buffalo, birds, and felines.

Image makers and spin masters have done an admirable public relations job at creating a positive connection between reptiles, mammals, and birds. The natural life-and-death process, the constant ebb and flow that exists between predator and prey, are now being viewed by many people for exactly what it is—nothing more, nothing less.

Television viewers in Europe, Scandinavia, and Great Britain tend to see the same programs on Animal Planet, the Discovery Channel, and other animal-themed channels as viewers in the United States and Canada. Public awareness has accordingly increased in conjunction with expanded activity in governmental protection, which begins with crocs and extends into entire ecosystems and their collective and varied inhabitants.

Deep-pocketed, thrill-seeking tourists are providing not only a boon for crocodilians, but also a financial impetus and incentive for national-level economies. Hopefully, these tangible rewards for croc conservation will eventually filter down to the often-impoverished inhabitants of villages. They are the ones who invariably bear the brunt of crocodile attacks.

Volunteer programs are in place in many sub-Saharan African countries that allow individuals to work (for a substantial fee and under strict supervision) with crocodiles in reserves and national parks situated throughout the continent. Education works in tandem with conservation. But the bottom line is money—and money talks just as loudly in Africa as it does anywhere else in the world. When people realize there is cash to be made from the conservation of crocodiles (as opposed to illegal hunting, trapping, and the selling of meat and hides), positive things start to happen.

The following is a sampling of various conservation efforts currently under way in Africa.

Uganda

In Uganda, a grant from the Captive Breeding Committee of the British Herpetological Society is being used to promote the well-being, welfare, and preservation of crocodiles, especially the Nile crocodile. One of the poorest countries in Africa, Uganda has only one crocodile farm located on the edge of Lake Victoria, about an hour's drive from Kampala. Uganda is also the source of the Nile River.

A crocodile workshop to promote the health, welfare, and conservation of crocodiles provided an opportunity to devise practices and regulations which will enhance crocodile conservation and the reptile's status in the wild. Since 1971, when the IUCN/SSC Crocodile Specialist Group was formed, the status of sixteen of the world's twenty-three croc species has been demonstrably enhanced by ensuring that all crocodilians have monetary and tangible benefit to those who live in proximity to them.

The workshop consisted of members of the Uganda Wildlife Authority, the Department of Wildlife and Animal Resources Management of the Faculty of Veterinary Medicine, Makerere University, research workers, and crocodile farmers.

The Uganda Wetlands Program is an effort to manage and protect the nation's wetlands, which comprise 13 percent of the country's surface area. Wetlands are also an important crocodile habitat.

Gabon

The wetlands between Lambarene and Port Gentil in Gabon's Ogooue Delta, the second-largest freshwater delta on the African continent, is being proposed as a Biosphere Reserve. In addition to crocodiles (which would enjoy a higher level of protection than is now afforded them), the area in and around Lambarene—where Nobel peace prize winner Albert Schweitzer lived, worked, and died—would also be granted more protection.

Nigeria

Conservation strategies have been recommended by experts for Nigeria, the most populated country in Africa. The Nile crocodile and the African slender-snout are seriously threatened in southeastern Nigeria. Rapid, unchecked human population growth and an increasingly degenerative economic situation compel people to misuse natural assets.

As a result, an exorbitant number of crocodiles are killed annually for the production of a variety of leather goods and local consumption. Recommendations to rectify the situation include the establishment of operating farms for the sustainable cultivation of crocodilian resources, a better understanding of the remaining crocodilian population, and the creation of protected areas in the Niger Delta and coastal lagoons.

Nigerian Decree Number 11 (dated 1985) states that the "hunting or capture or trade in the animal species listed in Schedule 1 is absolutely prohibited." The Nile crocodile and the dwarf or broad-snouted crocodile are listed, but the slender-snout is not. The Nigerian CITES Management Authority contends the ban is still in effect. Enforcement of the ban is lacking, no doubt due to the unstable political situation in the country and the lack of financial resources.

Skulls of slender-snouted crocodiles have been found in the "ju-ju" (traditional medicine markets) in Calabar, capital city of the Cross River State.

Ghana

Ecotourism has come to Grupela, a small village in Tamale, a northern region of Ghana. After a large crocodile attacked (but did not kill) three children and a dog who ventured too close to a pond where the reptile resided, villagers were understandably panic-stricken. People and crocs in Grupela have lived in harmony for over 100 years. The largest Nile croc in the local population is estimated to be around thirty years old. It had become so habituated to people over the years that locals in the past swam, bathed, washed, gathered water, and fished within very close proximity to the animal without fear of attack.

As is so often the case, encroachment on the crocodile's habitat was blamed for the unprecedented assault. Because Grupela's crocs are regarded as sacred, it was decided that all things considered, the introduction of ecotourism was the best solution for the village. Taboos and religious beliefs notwithstanding, people were also advised not to splash around too much when in the water where the croc resided, and to be very careful when at the water's edge. Empirical-based caution often trumps religion, especially where potentially man-eating crocs are concerned.

Zimbabwe

In January 2006, *The Herald* newspaper in Harare, Zimbabwe, reported that at least twelve crocodiles had starved to death at a Zimbabwean croc farm. The Parks and Wildlife Management Authority, working with the Zimbabwe National Society for the Prevention of Cruelty to Animals, rescued 258 crocodiles that probably would have suffered a similar fate. The four-year-old reptiles were housed in four dry ponds, which caused serious skin damage due to lengthy exposure to the sun.

All crocodilians must spend long periods of time in the water. Not only is it their natural element, but they are also susceptible to various skin ailments invariably exacerbated by the blast furnace–hot African sun. In Africa, the need to remain in an aquatic environment forces crocodiles to sometimes share their habitat with hippos.

The two species have, over thousands of years, established and maintained an uneasy truce. They avoid contact with one another as much as possible. Hippos will attack any animal that gets too close to the herd, and an adult is more than capable of killing a crocodile.

For their part, crocodiles rarely attack fully grown hippos, although they have been known to go after babies and juveniles. Dead hippos provide an easy meal for crocodiles, and the consumption of large, rotting corpses helps to clean rivers of pollutants and maintain their environmental integrity. In this respect, crocodiles and hippos have a somewhat symbiotic relationship in which both species profit.

The farm where the sick crocodiles were kept is owned by the chief executive of the Zimbabwe Tourism Authority, Kanikoga Kaseke. Kaseke told the newspaper he had been offered the farm under President Robert Mugabe's questionable land reforms, in which the government confiscated all white-owned commercial land (including wildlife sanctuaries) and awarded them to black farmers. Critics contend that many recipients lack the requisite competence to take on prosperous game-farming enterprises.

South Africa

A water supply scheme in KwaZulu-Natal, South Africa, will protect both people and crocodiles. Over the past fifteen years, at least sixteen people, mostly women, have been attacked by crocs when fetching water from the Nyalazi River. To prevent such attacks in the future, a mobile water treatment plant was established near the river, and will pump water to five reservoirs in the Nkundusi area near Mtubatuba. This project was valued at 1.3 million rand ($212,305 in U.S. dollars).

Also in KwaZulu-Natal, a plan is under way to eradicate an invasive plant species called *Chromolina*, which shades nesting sites and negatively influences incubation of crocodile nests in the 134-square-mile St. Lucia system. The plant's extensive root system also greatly inhibits the nest construction efforts of female crocs.

The current crocodile population, estimated at about 800 mature males and females, already faces threats from poaching, habitat eradication, fractiousness with livestock production, and competition with people for existing natural resources. The Nile crocodiles are a keystone species in the St. Lucia system because they control the fish population and clean up the system by eating dead hippos.

The KwaZulu-Natal Conservation Services have reduced the number of croc eggs that are annually collected for research, closed a popular hiking trail that led through breeding areas, and increased the number of game guard patrols. Furthermore, a Nile crocodile action plan group has been initiated within the Parks Service to continue various administrative and preservation projects for crocodiles.

Officers in the St. Lucia Crocodile Center removed a 13-foot (4-meter) crocodile weighing 771.6 pounds (350 kilograms) from the Mallanjack Estates in the Nkwalini Valley and relocated it to the Dumazulu Kraal and Lodge, a croc farm, where it no longer posed a danger to human life. Eight other large crocs were also removed. Officers used syringes attached to long poles to tranquilize the animals before their mouths were tied tightly shut and their eyes padded to reduce stress on the animals. Then they were laboriously and very carefully dragged out of the mud and reeds to a flatbed truck, which took them to their new home.

Live exports of Nile crocodiles to China by one farm were suspended due to a high mortality rate of the crocs in transit.

Tanzania

The vice chairman of the Crocodile Specialist Group for Africa recently offered technical assistance to Tanzania's Wildlife Division of the Ministry of Natural Resources and Tourism, on issues relating to the need to control problem crocs near human habitation centers. Control measures were recommended, including: restricting problem crocodile harvesting from the wild to areas of human occupation (excluding national parks and game reserves), and minimizing size limits.

They still face obstacles, such as how to direct the profits from crocodile use to regional locales, and how to generate different options for crocodile removal, to decrease loss of human and cattle lives and harm to fishing nets.

A Trade in Endangered Species (TED) study (Case Number 208) reported that some Tanzanian natives use crocodile parts such as teeth and claws for decorations on ceremonial accessories, as part of their culture. Crocodile meat is readily eaten by many people in different parts of Tanzania, and crocodiles have been used for meat and meat products for human consumption outside of tribal Africa.

Skeletal bones and osteoderms of the crocodile are being used for nutritional supplements in agricultural and animal feeds, and teeth and claws are being sold primarily to tourists as souvenirs. Crocodiles have also been used for medicinal purposes. The body fat and oil of crocodiles is believed by many people to cure skin ulcers, burns, and respiratory ailments.

The news of the healing powers of crocodile fat has spread to other countries, and the demand for these medicines is increasing. It has already been reported that recent outbreaks of crocodile poaching in the Dominican Republic and Haiti are related to the use of crocodile fat as a folk remedy for asthma.

■ ■ Between the years 1950 and 1980, it was estimated that around 3 million crocodiles worldwide were killed for their skins. Populations of the Nile crocodile are being conserved and encouraged where they do not conflict with legitimate human interests. The aims of the Nile crocodile management program are: to maintain and increase their overall numbers to produce a sustainable harvest; to regulate and control their numbers, where appropriate; and to manage the crocodiles for the benefit of local communities.

The conservation of the Nile crocodile has been difficult, due in part to the fact that many people are not fond of crocodiles. In Tanzania and other African countries, they cause extensive property damage and loss of life, both livestock and human.

The farming and/or ranching of Nile crocodiles, legalized under Tanzanian law, has led to a decrease in illegal trading activity, and has provided a new perspective on the crocodile, leading to increased protection for the wild populations. The increase in quality Nile crocodile skins from ranching and farming is helping to answer the demand for skins, and enhancing the supply currently obtained from the wild (both legally and illegally). Nile crocodile skins are regarded as being arguably the finest in the world, because they do not have a preponderance of osteoderms that can create blemishes and reduce commercial and aesthetic value.

Nile crocodiles have not been traded as live species yet. Some ranching operators have wanted to export live crocodile specimens for trade, but the recipients canceled the orders. It appears that ranching operators could receive a greater profit if they engaged in the export of live crocodiles.

A demand for live, adult crocodiles exists for breeding purposes from countries outside of Tanzania that have established captive breeding farms. The price for a live crocodile is around $1,000 (U.S.), compared to the $200 to $300 for crocodile skins from dead crocodiles. If shipment of live Nile crocodiles commences, TED experts believe the species could become extinct.

The IUCN lists the Nile croc as "Low Risk, Least Concern." Significant populations exist in Botswana, Ethiopia, Kenya, Zambia, and Zimbabwe. However, for most African countries, there is insufficient data on the current states of Nile croc populations. The species no longer exists in Israel, Comoros, and Algeria, three countries at the edge of its range. The disappearance in Algeria and Comoros may be due to climate change and the resulting loss of wetland habitats. A plan to reintroduce Nile crocs into Algeria has been shelved for the foreseeable future because of continuing civil unrest.

Madagascar

The Nile crocodile brought attention to itself in Lac Ravelobe, Ankarafantsika Special Reserve, Madagascar, when an inordinate number of people near the village of Ampijoroa were attacked and killed.

International croc experts recommended the following measures:

1 Establish defensive barriers at the lake's edge on two water levels to allow for bathing and washing;

2 Encourage ecotourism, with easy and safe croc watching that hopefully would bring economic benefit to the village;

3 Install wells as an alternative source of water;

4 Provide easy-to-understand caution signs along the road leading to the lake and at the water's edge, to advise everyone (including and perhaps, especially) tourists of the threat presented by the presence of large crocs;

5 Prohibit net fishing in the lake (which contributes to over-fishing, and is also used by croc poachers);

6 Reinforce native beliefs, which regard the crocodiles as holy animals;

7 Start local outreach procedures that encompass the training of crocodile guides and data collectors, to gather information on human-crocodile interactions and ecological observations;

8 Support community-based conservation enterprises, discussions, and the inclusion of citizens in all stages of the decision-making mechanism; and

9 Consider the elimination of conceivably life-threatening large crocs from places of human activity as a last resort.

Malawi

Wildlife managers in the Lower Shire River in Malawi have advocated addressing local people's attitude toward crocodiles. A proposed plan would allow communities to share in the profits derived from croc harvests in return for their taking part in crocodile control.

In an effort to reduce crocodile attacks, the Zambezi Basin Wetlands Conservation and Resource Utilization Project, an IUCN project supported by the Canadian International Development Agency, has launched a public awareness crusade through meetings, dramatic presentations, radio broadcasts, and other communication techniques.

Also being promoted is the use by fishermen of larger, more stable boats that are not as susceptible to crocodile attacks as smaller watercraft, and the removal of aquatic weeds that provide excellent hiding places for crocs, and from which they often launch their attacks on people. Managers are being encouraged to preserve crocodile habitats by recognizing the precise areas needed for different phases of the crocodile's life cycle.

Ethiopia
Despite years of civil war and internecine friction, crocodile populations are relatively healthy in the majority of Ethiopia's rivers. The government-owned crocodile farm in Arba Minch is still operating, but will probably be shut down in the near future due to a lack of funds.

Rwanda
Rwandan wildlife officials were approached in early 1999 about the prospects of farming crocodiles. Rwanda intended to obtain their stock of breeding males and females from neighboring Uganda.

Kenya
The Kenyan Wildlife Service actively monitors wild crocodile populations and problem crocs. As the wild population increases, so do conflicts with humans. The principal problem section in the country is Lake Turkana, where the shoreline has been split up into fishing concessions. There has been an apparent effort to intentionally decrease the crocodile population from earlier levels by poaching and illegally killing the crocs.

Four crocodile farms remain open, and through a cash incentive, there has been considerable success in promoting local custodianship and egg collection for the farms, especially along the Tana River.

Lake St. Lucia is becoming increasingly saline due to the removal of the water for irrigation purposes upstream, making the lake a less hospitable environment for crocodiles. Fishing with gill nets, a common practice, is entrapping many crocs underwater, causing them to drown.

Mozambique

Subsequent to increasing political stability, Mozambique is becoming more active in crocodile conservation. In 1999, 350 problem crocs were culled and their skins exported. However, some were small and had a belly width of 7.8 inches (20 centimeters), implying the harvest was inadequately regulated. There have been persistent reports of eggs and hatchlings being transferred from Lake Korabassa to South Africa.

Ivory Coast

The Caooe National Park in the Ivory Coast is one of the few places where all three species of African crocodile—the Nile, the slender-snout, and the dwarf—are present. In 1983 the park was listed as a Natural World Heritage Site, but in 2003 that designation was changed to World Heritage Site in Danger because of fires, rampant, uncontrolled poaching, overgrazing, and the breakdown of management structure due to civil unrest.

In addition to crocs, eleven species of monkey (including baboon, diana monkey, black-and-white colobus, and green monkey) are found in the park. Also living in the park are: aardvark, lions, leopards, elephants, warthogs, seventeen species of carnivore, antelope, savannah buffalo, roan antelope, ten species of heron, six West African species of storks and ducks, and five of the six species of West African vultures, hawks, plovers, francolins, and black-winged stilts.

The park's 310 miles of tracks are only accessible during the dry season, between November and April. There are two tourist zones within the park for short- and long-term visits. An expensive but popular safari lodge is in Kafola, and there are hotels in Kakpin and Ganse. The park is one of the largest protected areas in West Africa.

In spite of civil unrest, a management/conservation plan has been introduced, with help from the Worldwide Fund for Nature and the European Union. Five checkpoints and seventeen patrol posts at 12- to 18-mile (20- to 30-kilometer) intervals are located around the park's boundary. The staff includes one director, six assistant wardens, and forty-six guards. The presence of the blackfly, which causes river blindness, has tended to discourage settlement and encroachment in the park.

Crocodiles (and leopards) have been exploited for their skins in the 1,275-square-mile Tai National Park in the Ivory Coast. In addition to a small buffer zone, the park adjoins another 280-square-mile wildlife reserve. Spearheaded by the World Wildlife Fund (WWF) and the Economic Community of West African States, measures are being taken to protect the forest.

Botswana

The Okavango Delta is Africa's biggest and arguably prettiest oasis, and supports distinctive aquatic and semiaquatic fauna and flora. Because it is a keystone species, the Nile crocodile aids in maintaining a complex equilibrium within this delicate ecosystem; this reptile is integral to the husbandry of biodiversity in the delta.

Recently, a project was initiated to train Botswanian and South African students in the field of crocodile conservation. Currently, there is no administrative strategy in place for the Nile crocodiles. Human activity is expanding, with connected and associated contamination; crucial habitat is being lost, and vital fish reserves are diminishing. The plan for the venture was presented to the Office of the President by way of the Kalahari Conservation Society, and was accepted in March 2001. The project began in January 2002.

The particular goals of the project are:

1 to find out how many Nile crocodiles live in the Okavango delta and river system;

2 to create a database detailing the dispersal of crocs and their home ranges;

3 to maintain the well-being of the breeding population, determining the diet, feeding habits, and mating tactics of the breeding crocodiles;

4 to verify the magnitude and implications of human-crocodile friction within the area;

5 to collect important data on crocodilian parasites;

6 to generate local proficiency in all areas relating to crocodiles;

7 to aid Botswanian crocodile farmers;

8 and to emphasize the conservation implications of the survey, giving management advisements to the Botswanian Department of Wildlife and National Parks.

This is the first scientific and monitoring program on Okavango Nile crocodiles in over fourteen years. The biological data gathered will aid crocodile farmers in Botswana in enhancing sustainable farming procedures. The increased monetary significance of farmed crocodiles will lead to more effectual crocodile preservation in the Okavango Delta.

CHAPTER ELEVEN

ASIA AND THE FAR EAST: SUICIDE AND SALTIES

■ ■ Six crocodilian species are found throughout Asia and the Far East. Scattered over vast areas of often impenetrable, dank forests that are dominated by towering tree canopies, swamps, river inlets, and coastal tidewaters, crocodiles have over the millennia carved out specific niches for themselves. While it is true that several species may indeed inhabit the same country, crocodilians have very habitat-specific needs.

As a result, it is very rare (but not unheard of) to find more than one species sharing the same habitat. The art of adaptability, perfected over millions of years, is one of the major contributing factors in the crocodilian success story. The same species of crocodiles will compete with one another within a given habitat for territory, food, and mating privileges, but it is very rare for crocodiles to venture into another species' habitat.

Given the nature of their preferred environment—namely, isolated, inhospitable swamps, lagoons, wetland forests, marshes, and so on—historically, there has been more than enough room for individual members of each species to go about their daily business in relative peace. However, the often-unchecked growth of human population leads to problems. The accompanying expansion and increasing excursions into crocodile habitat—in search of arable land or tangible resources, such as fish and timber—have dramatically altered the relationship between croc and man.

Both species have suffered as a result.

Crocodiles, specifically their hides, were discovered to be a valuable commodity and resource well worth the arduous and hazardous treks into distant, often disease-ridden environments, fraught with many dangers. Crocodile meat can be smoked, preserved, and either sold or eaten. The latest development is the sale of alligator and crocodile trinkets and curios, such as bleached skulls, back scratchers, stuffed heads and stuffed hatchlings, paperweights, and similar objects sold as souvenirs.

The increasing demand for crocodile-related products has spurred technological developments and improvements in processing, tanning, and distribution facilities. Many farms and ranches located throughout the world are very profitable enterprises. The commercial reproduction of crocodilians has in many instances led to greater protections for wild populations.

Habitat destruction, unchecked human population growth (frequently in countries that cannot economically support such growth), and overfishing have increased the number of encounters between man and croc. Usually bad things happen as a result. More people get eaten or maimed, and crocs are forced to either defend their territory or retreat to more distant reaches of their habitat. Conservation and education efforts have tried, in many instances, very successfully, to make it easier for man and croc to coexist within the same territory.

It is yin and yang.

THE PHILIPPINE CROCODILE

Dispersed over the vast archipelago that defines the Philippines, the eponymously named Philippine crocodile is rapidly decreasing in numbers. The name *Crocodylus mindorensis* is derived from Mindoro Island in the Philippines (*mindoro* plus *ensis*, for "belonging to").

For all intents and purposes, the Philippine crocodile has been eradicated from Jolo, Masbate, and Luzon. It perseveres as secluded individuals and tiny populations in Mindanao, Negros, and Mindonoro. Confirmed sightings have also been verified in Nabunturan, Calarian Lake, Macasendy marsh, Liguasan marsh in Mindanao, and the Pagatban River in Negros. The species is also found in the Dipuyai and Busuanga rivers on Busuanga. However, the only population of any consequence is found in the one officially protected area, the Naujan Lake National Park.

Mainly restricted to freshwater areas such as small lakes, ponds, riverine tributaries, and marshes, the wild population is estimated to be between 200 to 500. This population is rated as "Critically Endangered" by the IUCN Red List, and faces the very real possibility of extinction.

The initial decline was caused by hunting for their hides and meat. Massive habitat invasion by humans, and horticultural programs to feed unchecked numbers of people, have exacerbated the problem, to which there seems to be no viable solution. The Crocodile Specialist Group is of the opinion that the Philippine crocodile is arguably the most threatened of all crocodilian species in the world.

Male Philippine crocs are relatively diminutive, rarely growing larger than 10 feet; females are smaller. Their diet consists mainly of small vertebrates and aquatic invertebrates.

The Crocodile Farming Institute, operated by the Philippine government, is breeding the croc for money-making and conservation purposes. The Gladys Porter Zoo in Brownsville, Texas, is also breeding the croc, and has sent hatchlings to the Philippines. A public education program has been formed by the Melbourne (Australia) Zoo. Captive breeding may be the only way to save this species.

THE NEW GUINEA CROCODILE

Crocodylus novaeguineae, aka the New Guinea crocodile (or the New Guinea freshwater crocodile) is a small- to medium-sized croc whose wild population is estimated at 50,000 to 100,000. Males max out at around 11.6 feet; females at slightly less than 9 feet.

Its range is Indonesia (Irian Java only) and Papua New Guinea. Freshwater swamps, lakes, and marshes are its favorite habitat. Unlike most other crocodilians, this thriving species rarely emerges during the day to bask, preferring to remain protected and hidden in covered areas. It is a nocturnal creature highly valued for its skin.

Illegal hunting and habitat disruption are the principal threats to the New Guinea crocodile. The IUCN Red List categorizes this croc as "Low Risk, Low Concern" because it is found in abundant numbers in its extensive habitat.

Large-scale ranching operations function in cooperation with local landowners to create sustainable harvests and egg collections of the New Guinea crocodile. In New Guinea and Papua New Guinea, commerce in wild hides is restricted to larger-sized hides. The aim is to safeguard the segment of the full-grown breeding population that surpasses those measurements.

THE MUGGER CROCODILE

The mugger or marsh crocodile is one of the world's true man-eaters. *C. palustris* comes from the Latin *palustris*, meaning "swampy" or "marshy," which gives it one of its common names. "Mugger" is a corruption of the Hindi word *magar*, which means "water monster." Oddly enough, given the number of crocodiles that live in close proximity to people, attacks are relatively rare compared to other species.

The mugger's habitat includes areas of Bangladesh, India, Iran, Nepal south of the Himalayas, Pakistan, and Sri Lanka, in freshwater rivers, marshes, and lakes. This croc has also adapted to live in irrigation canals, reservoirs, and other man-made bodies of freshwater in India and Sri Lanka.

Because its snout is the broadest of any member of the *Crocodylus* genus, the mugger has an alligatorian appearance, and like the alligator, it has enlarged scutes around the throat area that serve a protective function when they lumber through shallow-water, swampy areas.

The aptly named mugger has been known to migrate significant stretches over land to explore more agreeable territory. They max out at between 13 and 16 feet. Adults can weigh as much as 1,000 pounds. The estimated wild population is estimated at less than 2,500, causing the IUCN Red List to classify this species as "Vulnerable," primarily due to habitat destruction.

Adult mugger crocs are capable of taking down large mammals such as deer and buffalo. Humans pose no problems for a hungry mugger. Large fish, monkeys, snakes, and birds are staples of the mugger's diet.

A small population of mugger crocs, estimated at between 200 to 300, resides in the southeastern part of Iran. These crocs live in the Bahukalat protected area in the province of Sistan-Baluchestan, located near the Pakistani border, occupying natural and artificial water bodies such as dams, fish-farming ponds, and reservoirs.

It is a common practice to construct artificial ponds in general areas near villages to hold rainwater for people's daily use. In any of these ponds, one or two muggers can usually be seen, and their burrows are clearly visible.

The mugger crocodile species is also known as the Iranian short-muzzle crocodile, and is called *Gando* by local people. It is a large croc that can grow up to 16 feet in length. Due to religious and social beliefs, people respect the crocodiles and do not disturb them. By and large, they are regarded as being somewhat shy and reclusive by crocodilian standards. They prefer to hunt at night.

Sri Lanka has the largest population, estimated at around 2,000 crocs. They are consolidated in two national parks, Wilpattu and Yala. In Pakistan this species is extinct in the Punjab province, but small, unprotected and dwindling numbers are reported in Sind along the Nara Canal, in the Khairpur Sanghar and Nawab districts, and Lake Haleji.

Individuals are known or thought to be in the Mahakali, Nala, Karnali, Babai, Rapti, Narayani, and Koshi Nepalese river systems. River interferences such as damming, and fatalities in fisheries caused when the crocs try to catch snared fish, present significant difficulties for the mugger.

Between 3,000 and 5,000 muggers are present in India, but they are divided into more than fifty small populations. Captive breeding programs have been successful in India, but overstocks of captive-bred muggers are confined to captivity due to the fact that local authorities resist the idea of reintroducing the crocs into the wild. In a rare, almost unprecedented attack on people, a *Gando* killed a twelve-year-old boy in September 2003. The youth was swimming with friends in a conservation reserve when the assault occurred. The director of the local environmental office said it was a very uncommon and shocking incident, since the crocodiles were regularly fed fish, chickens, and even baby goats. Apparently this led the villagers to a false sense of complacency, believing that if they pacified the crocodile with these food sources, it would not attack them. Obviously, they were wrong.

WORKING WITH CROCODILES

Cleaning out crocodile or alligator enclosures is not particularly difficult. The reptiles are typically housed in large but relatively shallow pools, around 3 to 5 feet deep, that are in turn surrounded by a high chain-link fence or similar barrier. After the pools are completely drained by a pump, they are hosed down to clean out the fecal matter and food scraps that sink to the bottom. Floating debris (such as leaves) is removed with skimmers, and the pools are then refilled with clean water. Algae-inhibiting chemicals (and sometimes even bleach) are also added at the same time. Clear water makes for a better visual presentation, and also allows keepers to know where all the residents are at any given time.

There should be ample room around the pools for crocodiles and alligators to sun themselves and move around. As they regulate their body temperature, the reptiles go in and out of the water. Often there are bushes and trees in the area, which, if not an exact duplication of their natural habitat, at least provide a similar type of environment.

Unlike other large predators such as lions, hyenas, tigers, or cheetahs, crocodiles and alligators are not relocated to a separate holding area when their enclosures are being drained, washed, and refilled. I have drained, cleaned, and refilled pools containing fifteen to twenty 6- to 7-foot-long alligators, and the job took on average about thirty minutes.

These alligators were large enough to do serious damage if they had been so inclined. I was always aware of where they were in proximity to myself, and I never felt threatened or in any particular danger. As a rule, they simply moved out of my way. Standing at the bottom of a drained, 3-foot-deep, slope-sided pool, surrounded by fairly large alligators, could be a little unnerving for some, but once their habits and tendencies are understood, they are not quite as intimidating.

Like any other animal, alligators and crocodiles usually give warning signs when someone gets too close. They communicate with sounds such as hissing, and body language, including snapping of their jaws. On the other hand, their attacks are usually explosions of action and energy, and often, there is no warning unless the animal is already visible.

On land, a croc or gator may charge unexpectedly. In water, the animal will stalk, slowly cruising closer and closer. When it judges the distance to be to its liking, it will burst out of the water like a missile.

CROCODILE ATTACKS IN ASIA

In April 2005, Jamaludin Abdul Wahid, a thirty-seven-year-old zookeeper at the Singapore Zoo, nearly paid with his life when he let his guard down. He was far from ready when he was suddenly attacked by a relatively small, 5-foot, 7-inch-long croc while cleaning out the reptile's pen. The crocodile unexpectedly charged the inattentive zookeeper, who apparently was not agile enough to get out of the way. The croc sank a goodly number of its teeth into Wahid's leg, puncturing it in seven places.

"When the crocodile bit me, all I could think of was to get my left leg out of the crocodile's mouth," he later told an English-language daily newspaper as he recovered in a local hospital. Had the croc been larger, the story might have had an entirely different ending. Hopefully Wahid learned from his mistake.

Zoos go to great lengths to keep their animals safely separated from their visitors. Dry moats, water barriers, and fences are commonly used. Not all zoo animals are inherently dangerous to humans, but most are capable of inflicting serious injury, either by accident or design. Many species of parrots are capable of lopping off a finger, and even small monkeys can inflict serious bites. In addition to generating extremely bad publicity, escaped animals present the potential for costly lawsuits.

A female saltwater croc provided the residents of Hong Kong with drama, mystery, and diversion in 2003, when it eluded capture for an astonishing eight months. Nicknamed "Gucci" by designer label–preoccupied Hong Kongers, the 5-foot-long, 31-pound croc was first sighted in a muddy, contaminated waterway in the suburban New Territories in November.

John Lever, a celebrated Australian crocodile hunter (the *Crocodile Dundee* movies were based on his legendary exploits), was brought in to catch the slippery croc. He set numerous baited traps, and when he got close enough to Gucci, he tried to fire harpoons to shoot the animal with tranquilizer darts. Unfortunately, nothing worked. Occasionally the croc wandered close to nearby homes and apartment buildings, frightening residents and raising fears it would attack a human.

Apparently there were enough fish in the waterway to keep Gucci alive and quite happy. On at least one occasion, it managed to sneak into a trap, cleverly grab the food inside without setting off the trapping mechanism, and make a successful escape.

Television stations and newspapers had a field day covering Gucci's exploits, and the croc hunter's frustrated attempts to capture it. At one point the reptile reached star status and topped a popularity poll of Hong Kong personalities, winning six times as many votes as Hong Kong's chief executive, Tung Chee-hwa.

The entire search-and-capture operation cost Hong Kong taxpayers around $39,000 (U.S.). Despite the concerted efforts of local experts and the accomplished croc hunter, Gucci was ultimately captured by Ng Lo-tau, an elderly fisherman.

Officials speculated that the croc had either escaped from a farm in nearby China, or was a former household pet that had been discarded when it got too large for its owners to safely handle.

Gucci's new home is Kadoorie Farm, a wildlife care center, where a brand-new, purpose-built home was constructed to house the famous reptile. The enclosure is around 194 square feet. By comparison, a modest apartment in urban Hong Kong has about 300 square feet of living space.

Another reptilian escapee made beachgoers in Beihai City's Silver Beach in China's Guangxi Zhuang region very nervous. When a nearby abandoned wildlife park drained its crocodile pool and left it empty, one clever former resident managed to slither down a pipeline and make its way to the beach, where it terrified sunbathers and swimmers. Lifeguards immediately got everyone out of the water and struggled with the croc for three hours before subduing it.

Mugger crocodiles lived up to their name and reputation in 2005 when they systematically assaulted and brutalized the approximately 300 families that eke out a meager living in the village of Vermali on the outskirts of Vadodara, India. In a span of less than ten days in April, large crocs filled the villagers' collective hearts with fear and dread.

Chanchal Baria, a forty-five-year-old woman, was ambushed by a 7-foot-long mugger at the village *ghat* while she was washing clothes. A *ghat* is a broad flight of stairs that lead down to the banks of rivers in India, providing access for bathers and people washing their clothes or dishes.

Launching itself out of the muddy waters in typical attack mode, the croc grabbed the unsuspecting woman and tried to drag her into the river, where she no doubt would have drowned before being eaten. An eyewitness said the victim frantically grabbed a large rock and held on for dear life while the croc started to gnaw on her.

Hearing her screams for help, farmers (whose plots of land border the river) rushed to her aid and started to pelt the croc with stones. With one flick of its powerful neck, the reptile threw the victim to one side like a rag doll before making its escape into the murky waters. The intended prey suffered serious injuries, but was expected to make a full recovery.

Ten days prior, forty-year-old Jasubhai Rathod was also ambushed near the *ghat*. "I did not see or hear anything," he said later. "It came from behind and grabbed my waist." Rathod managed to escape, and miraculously suffered only relatively superficial puncture wounds on his back and waist.

Normally, the crocs had preferred to go after goats and cattle, but the recent spate of attacks had villagers very concerned. Animal activist Snethal Bhatt explained that March through June is the croc's breeding season, and because of that, the villagers would be well advised to stay away from places where the crocodiles congregate.

Whether or not the villagers took that advice to heart remains to be seen.

One of the most bizarre methods ever used to commit suicide took place on the outskirts of Bangkok, Thailand, in August 2000. A woman climbed over a 10-foot-high fence and jumped into an enclosure full of crocodiles at the Samut Prakan Crocodile Farm, Thailand's largest croc farm. It houses around 60,000 crocodilians of different species.

Somjai Sethboonwas, forty, left behind two suicide notes indicating that she intended to kill herself before she visited the farm. The victim's mother said her daughter had recently been complaining a lot about her husband, and was crying every day. Samut, Somjai's husband, said his wife told him she was going to have crocodiles bite her to death, but admitted he'd never thought she would actually do it.

Horrified tourists watched helplessly as the victim was dragged into a pond and systematically dismembered by around 100 crocodiles. Sethboonwas made her successful attempt at feeding time, when crowds of tourists were buying buckets of raw chicken parts to give to the crocs.

Sethboonwas was an unexpected treat for the ravenous reptiles.

Initially, the crocodiles ignored her, probably distracted by the screaming tourists. Then the victim swam toward the crocs and was finally attacked. According to witnesses, she grabbed the body of the first croc to bite her and hugged it in a ghastly embrace.

After the first croc bit her, the others immediately followed, creating a reptilian feeding frenzy. Tanet Virayaporn, a tourist guide who had the misfortune to witness the grisly event, said the victim did not cry or scream as she was repeatedly bitten.

It took the crocs about twenty minutes before they were sated. Only then did they allow workers to remove what was left of the victim. An autopsy showed that damage to the skull and brain was the cause of the victim's death.

If people want to see large crocodiles up close and personal, there's a much better (and safer) way to get cheek to jaw with the huge reptiles. The Cango Wildlife Ranch in Oudtshoorn, 280 miles east of Cape Town, South Africa, lowers thrill-seekers in an enclosed, steel-mesh cage (similar to those used in shark-cage diving) into a pool containing four large Nile crocodiles.

The crocs, being curious creatures, invariably circle the cage, looking for a way in so they can sample the tasty human inches from their jaws. No participant has been killed in this unique experience, which is guaranteed to get hearts and pulses racing and adrenaline pumping. The best part is that they also get to live to tell the tale.

THE SIAMESE CROCODILE

A much less dangerous species is the Siamese crocodile (*Crocodylus siamensis*), classified as "Critically Endangered" by the IUCN Red List. The estimated wild population of this 10- to 13-foot-long croc is under 5,000. Although its habitat is far-flung and encompasses parts of Thailand, Cambodia, Vietnam, Indonesia, Laos, and Malaysia (Sabah and Sarawak), the ecology of this freshwater species is poorly understood. It is believed that it is all but extinct, except for in Cambodia.

The Siamese crocodile eats mostly fish, amphibians, reptiles, and possibly small mammals, catching its food in slow-moving areas of lakes, swamps, and sheltered parts of rivers and streams. Illegal capture, habitat destruction, and death by getting caught in fishing nets are the principal causes of this species' demise.

This croc is extensively conserved and reproduced in captivity in Cambodia and Thailand, and to a lesser degree in Vietnam, the Laos People's Democratic Republic, and Indonesia. Because its skin is considered to be very serviceable for the international leather trade, business use and administrative oversight are feasible approaches to conservation. Compared to other crocodilian species, the Siamese poses a low-threat risk to humans, and is regarded as being relatively benign.

THE FALSE GHARIAL

Another croc listed as "Endangered" and possibly "Critically Endangered" by the IUCN Red List is the false gharial, or *Tomistoma schlegelii*. *Tomistoma* means "sharp mouth," derived from the Greek *tomos* for "cutting" or "sharp," plus *stoma*, Greek for "mouth," referring to the slender shape of the jaws. *Schlegelii* means "of Schlegel," referring to the Dutch zoologist H. Schlegel (1804–1884), who is credited with its discovery.

The false gharial inhabits Indonesia (Sumatra, Kalimantan, Java, possibly Sulawesi), Malaysia (Malay Peninsula, Borneo), and possibly Vietnam. It has possibly been extirpated in Thailand. The estimated wild population is under 2,500.

The maximum size of this croc is 16 feet. Although its elongated snout suggests it is a specialized feeder (fish), in reality, it is a more generalist predator and also feeds on insects, crustaceans, and mammals. Its habitat is restricted to freshwater swamps, lakes, and rivers. Very little is known about this species. Habitat loss primarily due to rice cultivation, dams and flood mitigation, drowning in fishing nets, and hunting for its hide have not been kind to this crocodile. The false gharial is one of the few croc species in which females offer no parental protection to their young. Captive breeding programs have been established in the United States and Europe.

THE AUSTRALIAN SALTWATER CROCODILE

The largest living reptile and arguably the most dangerous crocodile to man is the Australian saltwater crocodile, aka the estuarine crocodile (*C. porosus*). *Porosus* means "full of callosities" derived from *porosis*, Greek for "callosity," plus *osis*, Latin for "full of," referring to the rugose and bumpy upper surface of the snout in large adults.

The salties' (as they are colloquially called) range includes the northern coast of Australia, Bangladesh, Brunei, Myanmar, Cambodia, China, India (including the Andaman Islands), Indonesia, Malaysia, Palau (Caroline Islands), Papua New Guinea, Philippines, Singapore, Sri Lanka, Solomon Islands, Thailand, Vanuatu (Banks Islands), and Vietnam.

This is an ocean-going croc that has been known to travel over 600 miles from its home range. Single individuals have been seen off the coast of Japan and islands in the Indian Ocean. Barnacles have been found on the scales of a few stray individuals.

This is the croc that strikes fear into the hearts of people who live with or near it. It is answerable for the majority of attacks on humans. Adult males can easily reach behemoth lengths of between 20 and 23 feet, and tip the scales at over a ton (2,205 pounds). There are an estimated 200,000 to 300,000 salties in the world. The IUCN Red List categorizes the saltie as a species of "Low Risk and Least Concern."

Salties are the most widely distributed of all the crocodilians, and in their home range, they are feared more than sharks. In addition to its monstrously large size, it is noted for having a fierce disposition. Salties have a high tolerance for salinity, but can also tolerate freshwater rivers, swamps, and billabongs. A billabong can be a streambed that is filled with water only in the rainy season, a stagnant pool, or a branch of a river that runs to a dead end. Movement between different habitats occurs between the dry and wet seasons.

Salties also have a well-deserved reputation as man-eaters. They are the megabeasts that have been devouring humans since prehistoric times. This crocodile has killed nearly twenty people since 1971, and has injured countless others.

Although population numbers are healthy, the animal is dispersed over an immense expanse, including thousands of islands where conditions and trade are hard to observe or supervise. The saltwater crocodile has the most commercially valuable hide of any crocodilian. The principle threats to this species are unlawful hunting and habitat loss due to coastal development.

Thriving sustainable-use programs have been initiated in Australia's Northern Territory. People are provided with an inducement to conserve the crocs and their habitat by egg collection from wild nests. Compensation is dispensed to landowners. Hatchlings are then sold to crocodile farms for rearing and hide production.

In India, restocking programs are viable in the Bhitarkanika National Park, and a sustainable-use program in Papua New Guinea is also flourishing. The total population of salties in India is estimated at 1,000.

ATTACKS BY SALTIES

When the tsunami struck in December 2004 and flooded hundreds of islands, marauding crocs soon took advantage of the situation. Bus driver Radhakrishna Pillai survived for days on coconuts and bananas after the killer wave washed away his vehicle and all its passengers. As he was about to wade in waist-deep water to an Indian navy boat waiting offshore to rescue him, he fortunately spied a large croc swimming at speed toward him.

Pillai managed to safely return to shore, but saw the croc opportunistically grab a child by the waist and disappear with it under the surface of the debris-filled water. Like Hurricane Katrina that ravaged New Orleans, the tsunami gave hungry crocs a bonanza of bodies. There is no doubt they performed a gruesome public service by disposing of many corpses.

Upali Gunasekera, a Sri Lankan pensioner, was peacefully strolling in his well-kept garden near his house in Matara when the tsunami struck. The house overlooks both the sea and a river, affording spectacular views that Upali regularly enjoyed.

When the mountain-high wall of water rushed ashore, Upali was instantly washed away. He had the presence of mind to grab a floating, wooden stool with one hand and a chair with the other, until another wave knocked them from his grasp.

When he saw a large estuarine crocodile approach him, he thought he was going to be eaten alive. Escape was impossible. To his utter disbelief, the croc did not open its jaws. Instead it gently and steadily nudged him back to shore and safety. Upali recognized the croc. It had regularly visited his garden. Upali had never harassed the animal. Did the croc repay Upali's kindness by not eating him? The aged pensioner wasn't sure, but he was very grateful nevertheless.

■ ■ ■

Located in the mangrove forest in the coastal belt of Orissa, the Bhitarkanika Sanctuary is home to the largest concentration of estuarine crocodiles in India. The 106-square-mile sanctuary has protected the crocs since 1975, and since 1977 over 2,000 captive-bred reptiles have been released into the sanctuary. In 1988 the entire region was converted into a national park.

A report in the *Asian Age* newspaper in March 2003 claimed that upwards of 2,000 illegal immigrants from Bangladesh are posing a serious threat to the estuarine crocodile by illegally fishing for prawns, crabs, and fish along the creeks around the sanctuary. Motorboats used by the immigrants deplete and degrade the mangrove forest, which is a vital croc habitat.

Orissa is one of India's poorest states, and when the region was severely flooded several years ago, the sanctuary's crocs promptly took action. They strayed from their natural territories and ate two people in the Kendrapara district.

One of the most distressing croc attacks involving mass numbers of victims occurred at Ramree Island during World War II. The island faces the Burmese (now called Myanmar) coast. A thousand Japanese soldiers were encircled by British troops, who had created a blockade around them. Growing desperate, the Japanese soldiers decided to attempt an escape through a nearby mangrove swamp under the cover of darkness.

That night, the Japanese not killed by British gunfire were eaten alive by crocodiles. Almost impossible to see in the dark, hundreds of the hungry reptiles ambushed the hapless soldiers at will, and without retaliation. Witnesses aboard nearby British ships later described the anguished screams of horror they'd heard, as the soldiers were devoured by the feeding crocs. Only twenty Japanese survived to be taken prisoner.

■ ■ ■

Residents of the Kanganaman village in Angoram, East Sepik Province, located on the north coast of Papua New Guinea, were under siege in 2005 after crocs began to run amok on the Sepik River.

An unidentified man was killed in his house while he slept—appalling evidence that salties do indeed hunt at night. In September, a group of Seventh-Day Adventist Church members were paddling in a canoe on the Sepik River when they were attacked by a large croc. A witness later said that in a shocking display of strength, the reptile clamped its jaws around the canoe and pulled it straight down. Because the group was close to shore and the crocodile was preoccupied with the canoe, they were able to swim to safety.

A month earlier a single man from the village of Kamanibit decided to return home in a canoe via the same river, after dark. He was also attacked—this time successfully.

Farmers in Cambodia raise crocodiles for their skins. Crocs and gators are relatively easy to maintain, and the more they're fed, the larger they grow. Hides are often a valuable and much-needed source of income for indigent people.

In 2001, Siv Hong, a four-year-old Cambodian girl, was eaten alive when she accidentally fell into a pool containing between thirty and fifty crocodiles. Her grandfather, fifty-two-year-old Kart Lim, kept the reptiles on his farm in Kompong Thom province north of Phnom Penh, where he fattened them up, killed them, and sold their hides as a means of supplementing his income.

The unfortunate girl had dropped an insignificant article of clothing from a bridge that spanned the pond, and slipped and fell while trying to retrieve it. The grandfather, who witnessed her fall, bravely jumped into the pond in a futile attempt to rescue his granddaughter. He was also immediately attacked. His life was saved by a neighbor who distracted the crocs with a stick. The injuries he received were not life threatening.

Crocodiles, especially the larger species like the Nile and saltwater, are sometimes said to develop a taste or fondness for human flesh. When certain crocs repeatedly attack people within a given area, it does not necessarily reveal a predilection for eating human flesh; rather, it reflects the ease with which humans can be caught compared to other prey items.

Villagers in Xog-Ogaal, a small community in the Shalbeellaha Hoose region of south-central Somalia, were nevertheless convinced a croc was singling out people and having them for dinner when it ate three humans within a span of several days in July 2000.

As is frequently the case, rural residents who live (and die) far from any representation of the state in the form of police, game wardens, or militia, bear the brunt of croc attacks. The assaults lead in many instances to the promulgation of superstitious beliefs, or the attempted extermination of local crocodilian populations by enraged citizenry.

Tanjung Puting is the largest and most dissimilar example of vast, coastal, tropical heath-and-peat-swamp timberlands, which used to blanket much of southern Borneo. The area was designated as a game reserve in 1935 and a national park in 1982.

The best-known animals in the park are the orangutans, which achieved world renown thanks to the tireless endeavors of the Orangutan Research and Conservation Program, based at the Camp Leakey research station. The 1,174-square-mile park sits on a peninsula that juts out into the Java Sea, and is home to over 220 species of birds, numerous snakes and frogs, and two species of crocodiles, one of which is a man-eater.

Thousands of tourists visit the park each year, and in April 2002, Richard Shadwell, a thirty-five-year-old British citizen from Sutton (in Surrey) was one of them.

He had been traveling in Indonesia since March 12, had a good command of the language, and had visited Indonesia frequently in the past. On the day of his death, Shadwell was swimming behind a boat in one of the many rivers that striate the park. He was accompanied by two Canadian citizens. An Indonesian national was also in the water nearby, and when this man felt a large, bumpy object under the water, he immediately recognized it for what it was and shouted for the other three men to get out of the water as fast as they could. The Indonesian swam for his life.

Mr. Shadwell only had time to cry out briefly as the estuarine crocodile grabbed him and dragged him underwater. The two Canadians escaped unscathed. Nothing of Shadwell was ever found.

Every now and then a saltie misjudges its intended target.

Matthew Goodall, the teenage son of Australian missionaries, avoided being eaten by a saltwater crocodile while he was paddling his surfboard across a murky creek that led to a beach. The incident took place near the town of Jaya Pura in the Indonesian province of Irian Jaya.

Witnesses said the croc was almost 12 feet long. It launched itself out of the water unseen, unheard, and totally unexpectedly. Before anybody knew what was happening, the reptile clamped its jaws on Matthew's arm and surfboard, and immediately attempted to initiate a death roll. A saltie can spin 360 degrees in half a second. Its jaws exert 3,900 pounds of pressure per square inch.

Without knowing how or why, the lad found himself in the extremely unenviable position of being on top of the croc for a while, with the animal between his legs. For reasons not fully understood—but obviously greatly appreciated—the reptile released Matthew's arm, allowing the boy to make his escape. Miraculously, he suffered only minor wounds.

Villagers later said the same croc that attacked Matthew had previously killed five people.

DON'T BE A VICTIM

Can attacks be avoided? In most instances, the answer is *yes*. The *Outback Australia Travel Guide* has issued guidelines that can be applied whenever in croc country. The following has been adapted from those guidelines:

- *Always observe and be mindful of crocodile warning signs.* They differ from country to country. Make it your business to know what they look like.

- *Don't assume it's safe to swim even if there is no sign posted that prohibits it.* Deep, still, or muddy waters are often preferred crocodile (and alligator) habitat. Always stay well away from them. Rock pools and waterfalls are usually fine, but if you're not sure, stay out of the water. Ask first before you go into the water. Remember: just because a croc isn't visible doesn't mean it isn't there.

- *Stay away from the water's edge.* No matter if you are camping, fishing, or taking an evening stroll, maintain a safe distance between yourself and the water. A saltwater crocodile, alligator, or a caiman are all capable of lunging out of the water with lightning-fast speed.

- *Never stand on logs or anything else that overhangs the water.* Saltwater crocodiles and other crocodilian species can jump straight up.

- *Don't clean fish or discard fish scraps in the water.* You're only enticing crocs. It has the same effect as throwing chum into the water to attract sharks.

- *When launching boats, avoid going into the water if at all possible.* A lurking croc might find a dangling leg or arm irresistible. Never hang an arm or leg over the side of the boat. A crocodile can grab a hand or foot and easily drag an entire body out of a boat and into the water.

- *Don't feed any species of crocodilian.*
- *Always supervise children in crocodile habitat.*
- *Camp at least 50 meters (164 feet) from the water's edge.* There have been many instances where people have been attacked because they pitched their tents or lean-tos too close to the water's edge. Just because crocs and gators have short, stubby legs doesn't mean they won't walk a short distance if it means getting an easy meal.
- *Don't leave food scraps at your campsite.*
- *If you see a sliding mark where the grass has been flattened near the water, stay well clear of the area.*
- *Avoid places where native animals or cattle drink.* Crocs (and gators) know animals have to come to more or less the same place. It is a favorite ambush spot.

Even if all of the recommended guidelines are followed, there is still a possibility of getting attacked by a crocodile. People become complacent and are seduced into a false sense of security by the beauty of croc habitat, which is typically pristine and populated by other nonthreatening creatures such as fish, birds, or small mammals.

After a hot, sweaty day spent in a swamp, wetland forest, mangrove swamp, or other crocodilian environment, the lure of cooling off in an innocent-looking stream, lake, or river is hard to resist. Many victims no doubt believed that if they stayed close to shore in knee-high water, they would be safe. It is an erroneous assumption.

I have stood on lakeshores 10 feet away from alligators who were completely submerged in 2 to 3 feet of water. Gators (and crocs) are very difficult, if not impossible, to see. Because I kept a respectable distance, I was never attacked. That's how gators and crocs make their living—by becoming virtually invisible until the last possible minute, and by then, it's usually too late.

On several other occasions, while photographing alligators in slightly undulating terrain, I became so preoccupied with one gator that I nearly stepped on another that was hidden from view. Fortunately, nothing ever happened, and I was probably more frightened than the gator.

A coworker at the alligator park where I looked after the gators decided he didn't want to go to the trouble of opening a waist-high door in the chain-link fence that surrounded a large pool containing a dozen 4- to 5-foot-long gators. Without giving the matter much thought, he nimbly vaulted over the fence onto a space between the fence and the pool, where the gators were basking in the sun, and he nearly landed on top of an alligator. The reptile could have easily bitten him and taken out a large chunk of his calf. The gator chose to whack him with his head, leaving the man with a large, multicolored bruise and a racing pulse, but no serious injuries.

Like many animals, crocs and gators are stealth hunters, and they see, hear, and smell humans long before the human ever gets an inkling the reptiles are there. When in croc or gator country, never take anything for granted. Also remember that even the smaller ones can seriously injure and kill a human.

CROCODILE CONSERVATION

Many different programs have been established or are in the process of being instituted in the Far East. Wherever there are crocodiles, the IUCN, the Crocodile Specialist Group, and other organizations are reaching out in an effort to maintain and save different species that come under threats for a variety of reasons.

The following is a sampling of the efforts that have been initiated and carried out during recent years.

Nepal

In Nepal, attempts to save the mugger crocodile by ranching are under way. Local people, usually fishermen in the country's southern zone, will be allowed to collect mugger eggs and hatchlings and sell them to the ranching facility. When they become large enough to survive in the wild, they will be released.

Other crocs bred and reared at the facilities will be sold to private ranchers. Those ranchers make money by rearing hatchlings and selling their hides. Monies are also generated for crocodile studies and educational programs. This tactic deters poaching (at least, in theory) because permits will be granted to private ranchers only for the number of crocs they are known to have. Contrasted to hides taken from wild crocs, ranch-raised croc hides have a much-higher quality and bring more money in the commercial market.

Malaysia

The saltwater crocodile population is recovering in the state of Sabah, Malaysia. As late as the 1950s, the crocs were plentiful, and attacks on humans relatively continual. Overhunting reduced the population over the next two decades. Then the numbers began to increase dramatically. Crocs were discovered in smaller rivers, which were regarded as sub-optimal habitats. The larger animals (i.e., those over 13 feet) were deemed responsible for the corresponding attacks on people.

Since mid-2000, there have been more than six critical injuries or fatalities reported from at least three rivers in Sabah (Sg Paitan, Sg Kinabatangan, and Sg Kalumpang), in widely disconnected locales. Victims were typically attacked either early in the morning or in late afternoon, and included both adults and schoolchildren. Activities by the victims immediately preceding the attacks were bathing, fishing, washing, and swimming.

The recovery of the saltwater crocodile was credited to several factors. The croc has been afforded legal protection in Sabah since 1982 (with amendments to the Sabah Faunal Ordinance, 1967, and the Sabah Wildlife Conservation Enactment of 1997); in addition, steps taken by the Sabah government have helped, including the gazettement, i.e. special protection of the Kinabatangan Wildlife Sanctuary, which is prime saltie habitat. Because of educational efforts and more rigorous enforcement by the Saban Wildlife Department, most inhabitants of Sabah know that all crocs are protected by the law. Poaching has been substantially reduced.

The timber industry has decreased tangibly, thereby reducing habitat disruption and the river traffic that in the past helped to degrade crocodile habitat.

Colonization of some rivers by saltwater crocodiles has been attributed to land clearing in the upper sections of watersheds, which favorably altered lower portions of rivers. This means there was an increase in the number of shallow, muddy banks, shallower channels, and changes in fish fauna—developments that were advantageous to croc habitat. Possible areas of habitat appropriate for nesting sites have been increased due to enormous forest fires that occurred in 1983, 1986, and 1998.

In 1997–1998, the El Niño-Southern Oscillation weather event may have greatly decreased nest flooding, an issue that may have been responsible for many crocodile deaths.

Most of Sabah saw the withdrawal of established croc hunters because of the precipitous decline (more than 60 percent) in the prices for crocodile skins in Asia. Also, many villagers who had previously hunted crocodiles moved to larger towns and cities to take advantage of better job opportunities.

Sri Lanka

In May 2002, a crocodile training program was held for the wildlife managers of the Bundala National Park in southern Sri Lanka. The program concentrated on croc capture and relocation procedures. The program was funded by the National Geographic Society.

The Ruhuna National Park appears to be a safe haven for both the mugger and the saltwater crocodile. Outside protected zones, crocs are habitually exterminated by farmers as vermin, or for their skins. Inside national parks, they are secure from hunters.

Indonesia

Because the people of Indonesia have historically utilized crocodiles for an assortment of noncommercial uses, a survey was undertaken to monitor croc populations in the wild. It was discovered that over the past ten years, commercial usages of crocs have expanded, and might possibly become a danger to the population status.

Myanmar

Myanmar is the largest country in Southeast Asia. Evidence strongly indicates that populations of the saltie or estuarine crocodiles may be severely depleted. A survey of the Ayeyarwady Delta was undertaken to ascertain the status of croc numbers.

The survey concentrated on the Meinmahla Kyun Wildlife Sanctuary (MKWS), which is a 52.5-square mile island in the lower Bogale River. It was found that no more than ten adult individuals and no more than 100 nonhatchlings existed.

Loss of mangrove habitat has been one of the largest components contributing to the dip in the number of crocs and other wildlife in the region. In the 1980s, a 26,935-square-acre swath of forest was converted into rice fields. Fixed and floating gill nets are widely used by fishermen, and this also compounds the problem. Crocodiles go after the fish caught in the nets, get trapped, and drown.

Myanmar has a lengthy tradition of safeguarding wildlife, even though they collect young crocodiles for farms and ranches, and sell croc meat and export skins to Thailand and Singapore. Commercial hunting of crocodiles ended in 1994, and the Protection of Wildlife and Protected Areas law of 1994 gives considerable protection to crocodiles and stipulates rigorous punishments for infractions. The staff of Meinmahla Kyun Wildlife Sanctuary started a crocodile program in 1995 that aims to accelerate crocodile population rejuvenation. The program is based on egg and hatchling collection and reintroduction back into the wild.

India

After twenty-five years of protection, the saltwater crocodile population in Bhitarkanika, Orissa, India, is reaching standard mature size disbursement. That the presence of adult crocs constrains the gathering of subadults has been illustrated in recovering croc populations elsewhere.

During 1999, a winter census totaled 672 crocodiles (150 hatchlings, 146 yearlings, 160 juveniles, 144 subadults, 72 adults), which was slightly larger than the previous year's count. However, the number of attacks on people and cattle has also increased incrementally.

An attack occurred in 2000 at the Saltwater Crocodile Research Center (often called "the sanctuary") in Dangmal. The Center is encircled by rivers and creeks, and an 8.6-foot-long croc that had been freed earlier came into a freshwater pond situated on the grounds. The croc was regarded as being semiwild, meaning it was used to the presence of humans and probably associated them with food. Semiwild crocs or gators are often the most dangerous because they have lost their natural fear of humans and will readily approach.

An attendant who had worked at the sanctuary for over twenty years walked into the pond in order to wash some containers, including buckets and other items used to feed the crocs. The semiwild crocodile grabbed the man and dragged him to the center of the pond. Other attendants managed to free him from the croc's mouth while the reptile was chewing on him.

The unfortunate attendant suffered excessive bleeding from his left hand and chest due to the many deep puncture wounds (it was speculated that he might have been bending over when he was attacked). Although he was rushed to a local hospital, he died from his injuries while en route.

Compensation for croc attacks is a contentious issue among the residents of villages on the periphery of the sanctuary. If a person is killed or maimed by a croc, the Indian government pays the victims (or survivors) 2,000 rupees—the equivalent of 45 U.S. dollars. If a person is killed or maimed by an elephant, the compensation is 1 lakh (a lakh equals 100,000 rupees), or $2,253. Many people are tired of being told not to venture into rivers or creeks where they are obliged to go to bathe and wash. Instead, they want the government to put up wire fences to keep the crocodiles out of those areas.

The other side of the argument states that it's the people who should be relocated elsewhere. Nearly fifty villages are home to approximately 30,000 people who have lived in the area since 1936. Another solution put forth is the idea of maintaining a band of mangrove forests at least 100 meters (328 feet) wide along all the rivers and creeks that border farmed land and areas where humans live within the sanctuary.

In 2004 the prime attraction of the sanctuary was released into the wild under the "rear and release" program at the Dangmal Crocodile Research Farm inside the sanctuary. Gori (meaning "the fair one") is a white crocodile hatched in 1975.

Since birth the female croc has lived in isolation because of her extremely aggressive demeanor. Attempts by the Forest Department to breed her failed when she killed three potential mates—not an easy thing to do when you consider that male crocs tend to be considerably larger than females. Gori also lost an eye in the process of rejecting her saurian suitors with such extreme prejudice. Officials were of the opinion that since Gori was suffering from intense stress, releasing her into the wild might be beneficial. Helpful to the crocodile? Maybe. Advantageous from the villagers' perspective? Probably not.

Iran

Iran is taking measures to protect the Iranian short-muzzle crocodile, which has been pushed to the brink of extinction. The reptile, which averages 8 feet in length, is indigenous to Sarbaz, Kalat, Kajou, and Pishin lakes in Sistan-Baluchestan province. They are found nowhere else in the world, and there are around 300 remaining.

Ali Azadi, director general of the Agriculture Jihad Ministry's Office of Livestock Breeding, said Pishin Lake was the sole habitat of the short-muzzle croc.

The Iranian Department of Environment is preserving the gene pool of the reptile. Artificial breeding programs are not in use due to religious beliefs.

Bangladesh

A recovery plan was devised for the marsh or mugger crocodiles, living in a pond in a holy shrine, Saint Khan Jahan Ali Mazar in Bagerhat, Bangladesh. In 1970 there were eight adults and around thirty babies. In 2003, the numbers had dwindled to only two adult marsh crocodiles—one male and one female.

The plan included: capturing and testing the fertility of the female and the spermatogenicity of the male; returning one crocodile (now residing at Khulna Zoo but originally from the shrine) back to the shrine; bringing adult crocs and/or eggs from excess inventory being raised at the Madras (India) Crocodile Bank; and conducting awareness programs with the residents of Bagerhat.

Vietnam

Mr. Phan Viet Lam, chief curator of the Saigon Zoo, intimated in 1999 that a venture to reintroduce Siamese crocodiles to the coastal area of Can Gio near Ho Chi Minh City, and to the Nam Cat Tien National Park is under way. It had been thought that Siamese crocodiles had previously been exterminated from those areas.

Cambodia

Fauna & Flora International (FFI) and the Department of Forestry and Wildlife (DFW) of Cambodia have confirmed that as many as 140 critically endangered Siamese crocodiles are living in the Veal Veng Marsh in the remote Cardamom Mountains, in relative harmony with the Highland Khmer of O'Som, a minority community that not only respects the crocs but also bathes with them and prays for them.

The FFI and DFW are combining their efforts in a united program of awareness, education, research, protection, and habitat administration.

Twelve DFW staff members have received advanced instruction and training in croc biology and observation and management procedures. Nearly 100 miles of rivers and wetlands in the Cardamom Mountains of Kampuchea have been surveyed on foot for the first time. Eighteen previously unknown croc sites have been discovered.

In 2003, the indigenous inhabitants established borders and ordinances for Cambodia's first crocodile refuge in Veal Veng Marsh. Siamese crocs are highly sought after by poachers and corrupt crocodile farms throughout Asia. An adult is worth around 2,000 U.S. dollars on the black market in Cambodia, where the average per capita income is around $270 per year.

The Philippines

When a fragmented population of Philippine crocodiles was found in northeastern Luzon in 1999, a preservation organization was established initially under the auspices of the Dutch-founded Northern Sierra Madre Natural Park Conservation Project, implemented by Plan International. Since 2002, the Crocodile Rehabilitation, Observance and Conservation project (CROC) has been in charge of the program, with funding provided by the British Petroleum Conservation Program.

The CROC project is aided by the Cagayan Valley Program on Environment and Development, which is a joint research and education program of Isabela State University and Leiden University.

Thailand

A conservation project initiated in Thailand in 1999 encapsulates all the attendant problems associated with conservation work. Dr. James Perran Ross, a wealthy, shrewd, and conservation-minded businessman, established a crocodile farm without any government funding. He bought every captured and known wild crocodile in the country at a higher-than-average price.

Soon Dr. Ross had acquired not only an excellent population with a good genetic base, but he'd also decreased the chances that rival farms would be established. His point was that breeding separates the money-making process from the gains made through conservation.

The problems facing Ross's well-intentioned endeavor include: the availability of appropriate crocs for release; suitable habitat for them to live in; and once they have been released, stable protection mechanisms that will ensure their survival in the wild.

Ross has the stock, and Thailand's protected areas represent about 12 percent of the country. Most rivers and wetlands habitat are almost inclusively utilized for fishing conveyance and sewage dumping, but a few possible locations remain.

Once they are released, the crocs' future security is the largest test. People do not welcome the idea of large, potentially man-eating crocs being released where they fish, farm, and by necessity, have to go to rivers or creeks to bathe or wash. If the crocs do not directly impact human settlements, they have a chance.

CHAPTER TWELVE

GHARIALS: LONG-SNOUTED DENIZENS OF THE GANGES

■ ■ Perhaps the most unusual-looking crocodile in the world is the long-snouted Indian gharial, aka Indian gavial (*Gavialis gangeticus*). *Gavialis* is a corruption of the Hindi word *ghariyal*, which is a name for crocodiles. *Gangeticus* means "of the Ganges." *Gavial* is a misspelling of the word "Gharial," which refers to the Hindi word *ghara* (pot), a reference to the swelling around the nostrils of mature males.

The gharial's distribution is limited to the northern Indian subcontinent. It is found in very limited numbers in Bangladesh, Bhutan, India, Nepal, and Pakistan. Small populations exist in the river systems of the Brahmaputra (Bhutan and India), the Indus (Pakistan), the Ganges (India and Nepal), the Mahanadi (India), and the Kaladan and Irrawaddy (Burma).

The estimated wild population is between 2,500 and 3,500. The IUCN Red List categorizes the Indian gharial as "Endangered." Gharials prefer rivers with deep, clear, fast-moving water and steep, sandy banks, and deep pools that form at sharp river bends. They like to bask on the sandy banks and rocky outcrops, and the young will hide for up to a year in roots, thick vegetation, or branches in the water.

The gharial is a large, highly aquatic croc. Males can reach lengths of almost 20 feet and weigh nearly 400 pounds. Their characteristic snout (the longest of all the crocodilians) is 3.3 to 5.5 times as long as it is broad at the base. Unlike other crocodiles and alligators, gharials cannot move very well on land. They are incapable of high walking, belly running, or galloping because their legs are very weak and do not have the strength to lift their bodies off the ground. They can only slide on their bellies. Their rear feet are webbed, which greatly aids in swimming, and their tail is laterally flattened, which enables it to swim fairly rapidly.

Gharials are primarily fish eaters, although examined stomach contents occasionally reveal the remains of soft-shell turtles, birds, and small mammals. Gharials have between 106 and 110 interlocking teeth. They rarely if ever attack humans, primarily because they are physically ill-equipped to do so.

Muggers aren't as passive, and in August 2002, Bangarani Das managed to free herself from certain death when she was attacked in a Sunderbans creek by a 15-foot-long croc.

Bangarani was fishing when the croc locked its jaws just inches below her left knee and tried to pull her under the water. The fifty-six-year-old fisherwoman pierced one of the reptile's eyes with an iron hook, forcing it to release its grip. She and her husband had gone to murky-watered Wall's Creek with several other people to catch shrimp, which they intended to sell at a local market in Khetramohanpur in Pathar Pratima. Instead, Bangarani almost got caught.

She felt a sharp twinge in her leg and screamed as she was dragged toward the middle of the creek. Every time she tried to free herself, sharp teeth embedded themselves deeper and deeper into her flesh. By the time villagers realized what was happening and started beating on the croc with sticks and bamboo poles, the determined reptile was already going into a death roll. It was at that point that Bangarani stabbed the croc's eye with the hook.

She was unconscious when they pulled her out of the water. The mugger had shredded her flesh to ribbons, exposing flesh and bone. The portion of her leg below the knee had been reduced to a bloody stump. The victim was taken to a health center in South 24-Parganas' Pathar Pratima about 50 miles from Calcutta.

CONSERVATION

Nepal

In March 2003, Crown Prince Paras Bir Bikram Shah Dev, chairman of the King Mahendra Trust for Nature Conservation, released newly bred gharials into the Narayani River at Amaltari as part of a conservation program. The Chitwan National Park (originally a private hunting preserve for the personal use of the royal family) in Nepal launched the Gharial Conservation Project in 1978, with support from the Frankfurt (Germany) Zoological Society.

In 1981 the first batch was released with transmitters to monitor their movement. The park had already freed around 500 crocs into the Narayani, Babai, Mahakali, and Gandaki rivers. On average 500 gharials are set free each year. Their mortality rate is extremely high, and it is estimated that only around sixty wild and seventy released gharials exist in Nepal.

Even though the captive rearing program is regarded as a success, river pollution, dam construction, and fishing nets (both gill and seine, which entrap the reptiles and drown them) have negatively impacted the gharials, as have fishermen who kill them once they become trapped in their nets. An IUCN study revealed that only 7 percent of all released gharials survived.

A new conservation program was initiated in partnership with La Ferme aux Crocodiles from Pierrelatte, France, Conservation des Espèces et des Populations Animales, Department of National Parks and Wildlife Conservation of His Majesty's government of Nepal.

In addition to fishing, the major threats to the gharial are habitat loss and hunting. Their hides are used for various leather products, and the eggs are illegally collected for folk medicinal remedies. Added threats to eggs are predation by rats, jackals, wild pigs, mongooses, and monitor lizards, and also, monsoonal flooding. Males are also hunted for the aphrodisiac attributes superstitiously related to their snouts.

India

The gharial has been granted full protection since the 1970s. There are nine protected areas in India that are linked with captive breeding programs and ranching operations, where eggs gathered from the wild are reared and then distributed back into the wild. More than 3,000 gharials have been released through captive breeding programs. The wild population in India is estimated at approximately 1,500 individuals.

A Gharial Conservation and Research Unit has been founded at Tikarpartha in order to augment the gharial population by releasing hatchlings into the Mahanadi River (Satkosia Gorge). These releases, along with releases in the Ken and Son rivers, have not resulted in population increases.

Bhutan

The Nepalese Kashara Gharial Breeding Center in Royal Chitwan National Park in Nepal sent two of the reptiles to Bhutan for use as breeders. The Gharial Conservation Center in Bhutan has only four female gharials. The World Wildlife Fund in Nepal and Bhutan have cooperated for the past several years to expedite and foster ecoregion conservation in the two countries.

CHAPTER THIRTEEN

AUSTRALIA: SALTIES RULE SUPREME

■ ■ The IUCN rates the Australian freshwater crocodile, or Johnston's crocodile (*C. johnstoni*) as "Low Risk, Least Concern." There are between 50,000 to 100,000 of them living in northern Australia, and as their name implies, they prefer lakes, billabongs, and swamps, as well as less-salty upstream portions of rivers and streams. As a rule, they do not reside in habitats near the coast, where the water has a high salt content and they would be forced to compete with the larger and much more aggressive saltie. The "freshie" is a smaller crocodile, rarely exceeding lengths of between 8 and 10 feet.

When they want to escape into the water in a hurry, they are one of the few crocodilian species that can gallop and leap over rocks and logs at speeds that have been clocked at up to 10.5 miles (17 kilometers) per hour.

In comparison to the saltie, they are a relatively benign croc that rarely attacks people. But don't try telling that to a twenty-five-year-old tour guide in Kakadu National Park. In September 2003, the unidentified man was severely mauled and repeatedly bitten by a nearly 5-foot-long freshwater crocodile. Kakadu covers an area of around 7,722 square miles and is the second-largest national park in the world. Habitats within the park include rivers, mangroves, and floodplains.

One of the most popular attractions is the plunge pool, where visitors can seek welcome relief from the hot Australian sun. This particular tour guide was swimming with a group of sixteen tourists at the Maguk plunge pool (a natural water hole) at Barramundi Gorge, about 63 miles south of Jabiru, when he was attacked.

Witnesses said they shouted a warning to swimmers when they spotted the croc on one side of the hole, but it was already too late. The wily reptile had submerged and chosen the unfortunate tour guide as his victim. The guide fought for his life as the croc grabbed his left hand, before biting him on the chest. Somehow the guide fended off the relatively small croc with his free hand, discouraging it to the point where it finally released him. The guide was taken to Jabiru Health Clinic and treated for his wounds. Officials were keeping an eye on the croc, but said that neither the guide nor any members of the group had provoked the animal.

Freshies were given legal protection in the 1960s and 1970s. Their numbers are large and broadly dispersed. By and large, their habitats are unimpaired. Their skins have a relatively low commercial value.

While freshies can and do kill humans, the saltwater crocodile is the mega reptilian predator of Australia's northern coast. Weighing up to half a ton, these giants are an iconic symbol of the Land Down Under. All things are relative, though, and it should be noted that the saltwater crocodile is not the only way Aussies come to grief, as the following chart illustrates.

Cause	Number of deaths between 1980–1990
Croc attacks	8
Box jellyfish stings	9
Shark attacks	11

Cause	Number of deaths between 1980–1990
Lightning strikes	19
Bee stings	20
Scuba-diving accidents	88
Drownings	3,367
Traffic accidents	32,772

A study conducted by the Royal Prince Alfred Hospital in Camperdown, New South Wales, reported sixteen crocodile attacks in Northern Territory waters between 1981 and 1991. Four of these attacks resulted in fatalities. The majority of attacks (thirteen out of sixteen) resulted from victims swimming or wading in shallow water. Half of the victims were known to be affected by alcohol. Ten of the sixteen attacks occurred in failing light, or at night.

The survivors' injuries ranged from minor lacerations and puncture wounds to major abdominal, limb, and chest trauma. Death in fatal attacks was caused by transection of the torso and decapitation. Microorganisms isolated from wound swabs included pseudomonas, enterococcus, aeromonas, and clostridium species. The study concludes that most attacks could have been prevented by taking adequate precautions.

Another analysis in Australia found that 29 percent of the sixty-two attacks that took place between 1971 and 2004 had involved alcohol consumption by the victims. Nonfatal attacks increased from about 0.1 per year between 1971 and 1980 to 3.3 per year from 2001 to 2004. All fatal attacks involved water, and 81 percent occurred while the victim was wading or swimming. Also, the average size of saltwater crocodiles had increased during that time.

In the past twenty-seven years there have been just two fatalities attributed to crocodile attacks in Kakadu National Park. Tour guides can operate without any minimum training requirements, including first-aid training. In other words, there are no minimum standards. Visitors are basically on their own.

Statistics aside, saltwater crocodile attacks create attention-grabbing headlines.

Russell August Butel, fifty-five, owned a successful aquarium supply business near Vashon Head, north of Darwin. He was influential and well-liked within the industry. He was also an accomplished scuba diver who liked to combine his vocation with an avocation. In October 2005, that merger resulted in almost instant death.

Butel was collecting fish, coral, and sea cucumbers for his business, diving in Trepang Bay about 15 nautical miles east of Cape Don off the Cobourg Peninsula in the Northern Territory. It was later speculated that he'd probably been splashing around in the water—not a wise thing to do when curious crocs are in the area. They usually bring the kind of attention people can live without (or die with). Local residents are aware that crocodiles inhabit the bay and are understandably very reluctant to go into the water.

The 13-foot-long saltie lined Butel up, instantly went through the vectoring process that included estimating the distance to the target, and submerged. The croc tucked its legs close to its body to reduce drag and water resistance, and with a few powerful swings of its tail, began his silent, unseen attack, which encompassed a distance of between 328 and 656 feet (100 to 200 meters).

At the last second, when escape was impossible, the croc surfaced next to Butel, opened its jaws wide, and guillotined his victim's head off. In one horrible instant just before he died, the victim no doubt saw the gaping, tooth-filled mouth and the elongated, triangular-shaped tongue, right before the powerful jaws snapped close, exerting thousands of pounds of force per inch on Butel's neck.

The victim's headless body was found floating around a mile from the attack site at about 4:30 P.M. The assault was witnessed by the victim's horrified diving partner, a forty-one-year-old New Zealand man who immediately scrambled safely into a nearby dinghy. He marked the exact location of the attack with an emergency beacon and used a satellite phone to notify authorities. Divers said the victim was working in an area where there was a high risk of attack. Police said they would not shoot the croc.

The Kakadu National Park guide who escaped a freshwater crocodile attack was fortunate. A twenty-three-year-old German tourist was not so lucky.

Isabel von Jordan was killed by a 13-foot croc while swimming at night in a natural pool. Nine people had gone into Sandy Billabong at 11:30 P.M. as part of a four-day tour. It was hot, the moon was nearly full, and the water looked inviting. The victim's sister Valerie, twenty-one, later told the German diplomatic representative in Darwin that a tour guide had assured the group it was safe to swim in the billabong because it held only innocuous freshwater crocodiles who rarely if ever attacked humans.

It's a wonder they didn't notice the many conspicuously posted signs that warn of the eight adult salties that live in the billabong. It's their residence, and their buffet table.

Isabel and Valerie had come to Australia from Bali to call on friends who had been evacuated to a Darwin hospital after being wounded in the terrorist attack at the Sari Club, a popular Bali nightclub. Valerie said they left the club only an hour before the deadly explosion. On that occasion Isabel was very fortunate indeed.

A scant ten days later, however, her luck came to a screeching halt.

James Rothwell, twenty-four, a resident of Sussex, England, said he felt a croc brush against his leg. A few seconds later he heard the victim scream and disappear under the water. Then it was all over. It had taken less than a minute. Rothwell said he shone a flashlight on the water and saw two red croc eyes swimming away from the spot where Isabel had disappeared, and then, the blurred outline of a crocodile highlighted against the night sky.

Search parties worked through the night and finally discovered the German tourist's lifeless body about a mile upriver from where the attack had occurred. Park rangers had to harpoon the killer croc the following morning in order to convince it to release the victim's body.

Groote Eylandt, a remote Northern Territory island in the Gulf of Carpentaria off Arnhem Land, was the last place British-national Russell Harris saw on earth. The thirty-seven-year-old mines superintendent's lifeless body was found in September 2005 at the mouth of Eight Mile Creek.

He had been snorkeling with another man off rocks approximately 330 feet north of Picnic Beach. They became separated, and Harris was last seen about 65 feet from shore. Local police said a saltwater crocodile had been previously observed at the mouth of the creek where his body was discovered. The place of discovery was about a mile from where Harris was last seen alive. The croc apparently grabbed the victim from underneath and pulled him under the water, where he drowned.

Fifteen years earlier, forty-three-year-old Albert Juzelionas, a Telecom worker from Jabiru, had met a similar fate when he was killed by an 8-foot croc while swimming on Groote Eylandt. And less than a week after Russell Harris met his maker, a fifty-five-year-old man was killed by a croc while scuba diving with a friend on the Cobourg Peninsula (not far from Groote Eylandt) in the Northern Territory.

Sixty-year-old Barry Jefferies liked to fish. In August 2005 he found himself in the extremely unenviable position of being the catch of the day for an 882-pound saltwater crocodile.

Midway Waterhole on the Normanby River in Lakefield National Park, northwest of Cooktown in northern Queensland, is a popular place with locals and tourists. Famous for its scenic beauty, the area is familiar to tour operators. Lakefield is Queensland's second-largest park. It comprises 19,395 square miles (50,000 square kilometers) of savannah and riverine flats drained by large rivers, and contains magnificent wetlands that are home to water birds, barramundi, and both saltwater and freshwater crocodiles. In the dry season, rivers are transformed into a series of water holes; in the wet season the park is an inaccessible wetland.

There are twenty-one campsites that provide few amenities. Campers must be relatively self-sufficient and, it is presumed, fairly knowledgeable not only about the terrain, but also about the different types of animals that make Lakefield their home.

Jefferies and his wife Glenda were fishing at dusk from a canoe, enjoying life and being on the water, when the croc silently attacked him, grabbed one of his arms, effortlessly dragged him out of his flimsy craft, and killed him. His body was never found.

People familiar with the area said the croc, which was later killed by park rangers, was an old animal that had lived near this water hole (and others) for many years. Had the croc become habituated to people? Was it too old to hunt for its normal prey? Had it turned to humans instead, developing a taste for people? No one ventured an opinion.

Jefferies's wife Glenda later told authorities she saw the crocodile approach them before it submerged. It cleverly followed a baited fishing line up to the side of the canoe and then propelled itself up and out of the water. It lunged and expertly caught her husband, who tried in vain to fight the huge reptile off with a paddle.

During the process of dragging the ill-fated victim into the water, the croc capsized the canoe, which vanished into the water hole. Glenda Jefferies surfaced as the saltie was biting her husband to death. Knowing she could not save him and fearing the croc might turn on her after finishing its grisly task, she frantically swam to shore as fast as she could. It took her twenty minutes to drive to the ranger station where she raised the alarm.

Helicopters and boats were used in the ineffectual search for Barry. Torn clothing was found several hundred yards from their campsite, but no physical evidence of Barry was ever discovered. A large croc was shot and killed the following afternoon, but no human remains were found in its stomach. Was it the croc that had killed Barry? No one knows. (However, after about a week in a crocodile's stomach, human bone takes on the consistency of very rubbery gristle, so it's doubtful that the rangers shot the right croc.)

Tour operator Tom Rosser expressed surprise that the couple had taken a canoe into known crocodile habitat. Many conspicuously posted warning signs advise against doing such a foolish thing. He said that people have fished in the river quite often, but typically they're in at least a 14-foot or larger dinghy, which is wider, more stable in the water, and more imposing-looking to the crocodiles. A larger craft reduces the chance of attack considerably. Canoes are notoriously unstable even in calm waters. When they are assaulted by an animal weighing a ton or more, they are almost certain to capsize.

In defense of their territory, saltwater crocodiles will attack just about anything, and it doesn't necessarily have to be edible. Being in a larger watercraft does not guarantee immunity from an unprovoked and violent assault, but it does give the occupants a better chance of survival.

Kel Luscombe and Steve "Chilli" Pye were fishing 1.24 miles (two kilometers) offshore in Princess Charlotte Bay in October 2002 when their 14-foot-long aluminum boat was attacked by a 16.5-foot-long monster croc. The saltie used its head as a battering ram, and knocked the boat sideways for a distance of at least three feet, according to Pye. His partner, who has been fishing in the area for thirty years, added that the croc was probably larger than 16 feet.

"We spotted him 3,040 meters [1.89 miles] away, near a sand quay, and he kept pace with us for a while, then moved closer and closer before he reared out of the water and went for us. The noise when he hit was like a car crash and he nearly threw me out of the boat." The boat didn't tip over and the three men were none the worse for the experience.

A kayak is an even worse choice when venturing out into croc-infested waters. Pom Jason Lewis, thirty-seven, was traveling around the world in 2005. He made it as far as Cape York Peninsula when his luck nearly ran out. When paddling from the appropriately named Lizard Island to the mainland, Pom suddenly found himself being intensely scrutinized by two large crocodiles.

The attack came late in the afternoon as he neared the sandbank, where he intended to pitch his tent and spend the night before continuing his journey the following morning. The two salties silently slithered off the bank and into the water as he got closer.

Pom saw the crocs and didn't think much about it. He had seen crocs before, except this time one of them started following him. That had never happened to him, and it frightened him. Pom paddled as fast as he could in an attempt to reach the beach and the safety he assumed it provided, but the croc kept on closing the distance between them.

He finally made it safely to the beach, but the curious croc refused to go away. When Pom foolishly tried to drive the beast off with his paddle, his only means of propelling his kayak through the water was destroyed. He survived the night in spite of the watchful eyes of the patrolling croc. The next morning he used his satellite phone to call a seaplane, which subsequently rescued him. It could have been a lot worse.

Almost exactly a year earlier, eleven-year-old Hannah Thompson decided to take a cooling dip in Margaret Bay near the top of Cape York Peninsula, when she was attacked by an 11-foot-long saltie who figured it had just caught a very easy and tender meal.

Hannah's life was saved by Ray Turner, a famous croc hunter who providentially happened to witness the assault from his nearby boat. When he saw the croc grab the diminutive Hannah by her arm and start to drag her under the water, the fifty-seven-year-old Turner took immediate action. He launched himself out of his boat like a human bullet and landed on the reptile's back.

With complete disregard for his own safety (and life), he assaulted the attacking reptile. After Turner gouged the croc's left eye, the reptile lost his appetite for little Hannah and broke off the attack, although it continued to circle the boat that was now occupied by Turner and his intended victim.

The celebrated croc hunter took Hannah and the rest of her group to Haggerstone Island, where she was medivaced to Thursday Island Hospital. Although she suffered deep puncture wounds to her lower arm, Hannah made a full recovery.

Lakefield National Park is accessible only by four-wheel-drive vehicles, and is renowned for viewing freshwater and saltwater crocodiles in the wild. The vast majority of people who camp and enjoy other recreational activities do so without incident, although officials do urge visitors to exercise common sense when in croc country.

Saltwater crocodiles may appear slow and lumbering when on land, but that does not mean they won't venture out from their natural habitat—water—in search of a meal. Like their Nile counterparts in Africa, salties know an opportunity when they see one.

Just ask thirty-four-year-old Andrew Kerr.

Bathurst Bay is a popular fishing spot 155 miles north of Cooktown in the remote Cape York Peninsula, in Far North Queensland. The Kerrs and a group of friends from Brisbane were taking an annual holiday, camping at the same spot they had visited for the past five years. They were familiar with the area and all the different animals that lived there. What could possibly go wrong?

Andrew, his wife Diane, and their three-month-old son Kelly were peacefully sleeping in their tent on a beach in October 2005 when their pleasant dreams suddenly turned into a horror show. A 14-foot-long (4.2-meter) saltie that weighed 661 pounds (300 kilograms) snuck up on them and lunged through the tent at the ungodly hour of 4:00 A.M.

Diane later told the *Brisbane Courier-Mail* that after she heard a thud, she got up and looked through the netting on the tent door and saw an immense crocodile staring back at her. She woke her husband in a panic, and when he sat up, the croc charged him.

The marauding monster grabbed one of Kerr's legs in a viselike grip and attempted to drag him back to the water. Kerr's wife Diane held onto the bassinet that contained their son with one hand and her husband with her other hand and started screaming for help as loud as she could. The croc dug his heels into the sand and effortlessly pulled all three of them (including the bassinet) out of the tent.

Diane's shrieks woke the Sorohan family camping nearby. Mr. Sorohan later said they'd heard screams, so they jumped up and raced out of their tent. Andrew would not have had the chance to yell or do much of anything, as the croc had him in his mouth.

Alicia Sorohan, a sixty-one-year-old grandmother who tips the scales at a feathery 121 pounds (55 kilograms), probably thought the croc had gone after the baby. Without giving it a second thought, she jumped on the reptile's back. The croc immediately released its grip on Andrew Kerr, turned around, and smashed her face with its head, breaking her nose. Then it clamped its jaws on one of her arms, almost tearing it from its socket, and started to haul her toward the water. Her husband ran back to their tent to fetch an ax.

While he was doing that, the croc was still trying to lug Alicia to her certain death. Their son Jason, thirty-three, positioned the barrel of a high-powered handgun against the back of the croc's head and pulled the trigger, instantaneously killing the animal.

By the time Alicia Sorohan had reached Andrew Kerr and jumped on the croc's back, Kerr was already badly mangled. One of his legs was shattered, and his entire body was hideously perforated and slashed. Bits of flesh were hanging off of him. The tent floor was covered in slowly congealing blood. Andrew Kerr was as limp as a rag doll.

Other campers on the beach activated a Cospas-Sarsat beacon (an emergency position radio), whose signal was detected by two quarantine officers who were eradicating wild pigs in the area. The signal also alerted the Rescue Coordination Center in Canberra, which immediately dispatched a Queensland Park Wildlife Service (QPWS) helicopter with a medic on board to the scene.

After a ninety-minute flight, the QPWS chopper touched down and evacuated the badly wounded Andrew Kerr and Alicia Sorohan, taking them to the ranger station. On the way the pilot alerted the Royal Flying Doctor Service (RFDS). Another helicopter dispatched from Cairns was also en route to the park after stopping at Cooktown to pick up a doctor.

Kerr and Sorohan were given emergency treatment at the ranger station by the RFDS before being medivaced to the Cairns Base Hospital. A flyby of the area confirmed that the killer croc was dead.

The attack was subsequently investigated by the QPWS, which believed the croc may have been tempted to the area by fish and food morsels carelessly and inconsiderately discarded by fishermen.

Kerr underwent several operations and months of recovery time, but he survived the ordeal. His wife and baby son were unscathed. Needless to say Kerr and his wife were extremely grateful. Alicia's actions had saved their lives.

Alicia Sorohan spent two weeks in the hospital and endured months of physiotherapy. She lost the full use of the arm the croc chewed on, now badly disfigured, and her hand no longer rotates properly. In spite of her ordeal, Alicia continues to return to the same camping spot. She told reporters that she liked crocs before the unfortunate incident, and she continues to like them.

"They are fascinating creatures," she added.

The Finniss River is 50 miles southwest of Darwin in the Northern Territory. Although certain channels are only about 4 feet deep, they and most of the river can safely be navigated by large boats that are 14 feet wide. At its widest point the river is 329 feet across, and it's slightly less than 6 miles long. The river is prime saltwater croc habitat.

It is also possible to ride all terrain vehicles (ATVs) on broad, lush, verdant paths that run parallel to the river and follow its course as it meanders in a series of gentle arcs and curves in a north by northwesterly direction. ATV riding is a popular recreational activity in the area.

In late December 2003, tropical cyclone Debbie tracked south by southwest and dumped between 6 and 12 inches of rain over a large area, causing significant rises in water levels and local flooding as it skirted the Northwest Territory. The combination of Debbie, the Finniss River, and resident crocs created an unforeseen set of rarely combined circumstances that forced two young men to witness a friend being eaten alive.

Shaun Blowers and Ashley McGough, both nineteen, and Brett Mann, twenty-two, had been riding their ATVs parallel to the Finniss River for most of the day. The track, although muddy and full of potholes, was nevertheless navigable. All three of the young men were experienced, safety-conscious riders who knew how to have fun without taking unnecessary risks.

Their scheduled, day-long Sunday ride began uneventfully, and by afternoon they had parked their ATVs above the riverbank and were ready to go down to the river to wash the mud and sand off themselves and their clothes. Brett Mann left the safety of the sandy bank and ventured out a little farther.

It was a fatal mistake.

The recent rains had swollen the river and increased the speed of the current. Taken unawares, Mann lost his footing on the moss-slippery rocks and pebbles and was swept away. Blowers and Mc-Gough immediately jumped in and swam to his rescue. After they reached him, they positioned themselves in front of him, shielding him from the current. They were in the process of leading him back to shore when Blowers walked past a lurking, 13-foot-long croc. He didn't see the reptile, but McGough did, and yelled a warning. Mc-Gough and Blowers swam to the nearest tree and scrambled up the trunk. Mann was nowhere to be seen. There had been no splashing, no scream *in extremis*—no sound whatsoever.

A few minutes later the huge reptile surfaced with the lifeless body of Brett Mann firmly clamped between its jaws. It swam toward the treed pair as if showing them a trophy. Then it swam away, only to reappear approximately five minutes later. Brett Mann was no longer between its jaws. Apparently the croc had wedged the victim's lifeless body against submerged rocks or logs, where the corpse would no doubt remain for several days, curing.

In the meantime, the saltie was hoping to nab another victim. It cruised close to the tree, looking up, hoping one of the lads would fall down where he would be an easy catch. The persistent, patient croc hung around all night as Blowers and McGough clung to each other, shivering in the cold darkness. They were afraid to go to sleep while the still-hungry croc lurked below them. They knew the river was rising. Would the water level climb high enough to enable the croc to jump up and grab one of them? The saltie finally gave up and left the following morning. They had been in the tree for twenty-two hours.

When they failed to return as expected Sunday night, concerned family and friends called police, who immediately launched a search mission. They were finally discovered by a helicopter at 3:30 P.M. that afternoon and winched to safety.

Blowers and McGough were treated for exposure and shock at Royal Darwin Hospital before being released. Authorities used a helicopter, ATVs, and several dinghies when they searched for the remains of Brett Mann. Deteriorating weather later forced police to call off the search. Neither the croc nor Mr. Mann was ever found.

The river was also the haunt of a crocodile that became a legend in its own time, and after its untimely death, achieved iconic status in the Northern Territory. Nicknamed "Sweetheart," because it dominated Sweet's billabong (about 34 miles southwest of Darwin), this saltie weighed 1,720 pounds and reached a length of 17 feet. During the 1970s, the croc terrorized thousands of boaters for many years by ramming them and biting their propellers.

Because it was very territorial, the croc regarded any incursion into its domain as a threat, and it reacted accordingly, no matter how big or small the craft was. Scars lined its back and several teeth were chipped, evidence of several violent confrontations with propellers.

Wildlife officials used a tranquilizer dart to finally subdue the animal in 1981. Unfortunately, the drugged reptile sank to the bottom of the river, where it became snagged on a submerged log and drowned. Divers recovered its body and moved it to the Northern Territory Museum and Art Gallery in Darwin, where the remains are viewed by thousands of people a day.

About a week after Russell Harris and Barry Jefferies wound up as dinner for hungry saltwater crocodiles, another attack occurred. Ric Burnup and his children, ten-year-old Chantal and older brother Simon, were vacationing at Doubtful Bay off the Kimberly Coast, 218 miles northeast of Broome in northern Australia. Mrs. Burnup remained at home in Busselton.

They had rented a boat in the first week of October 2005. The family traveled by dinghy up an estuary to a water hole near the mouth of the Safe River. They were swimming and snorkeling for about twenty minutes when Ric saw his daughter suddenly disappear. What Chantal suddenly saw through her mask were the jaws of an 8-foot-long saltie, opening wide and closing around her.

Ric grabbed his daughter by one arm while Simon punched the croc in the head. The saltie, probably distracted by this unexpected retaliation, released its grip, enabling Ric to haul a very frightened Chantal to a nearby rock, where they saw that the croc was still watching them.

Miraculously, the cuts on one of her arms and a leg were not life-threatening. The girl was airlifted by helicopter to a farm at Mount Hart, about 150 miles northeast of Derby, where a doctor was to meet her. Later she was taken to Derby Hospital where she was treated for her injuries and released.

Another very lucky escapee is nineteen-year-old Manuel Pascoe. In November 2003 he was returning home along a creek near the Blyth River, about 250 miles east of Darwin, capital of the Northern Territory. Tired from hunting geese all day (and from the effort of lugging their carcasses home), Pascoe evidently forgot that crocs are very attracted to the smell of blood.

The 10-footer that lunged up from the bottom of the creek Pascoe was imprudently walking in probably thought he was in for a good meal—Pascoe *and* his dead, still-bleeding geese. What the croc could not have anticipated was getting punched in the snout by Pascoe's aunt, Margaret Rinbuma, who was hunting with Pascoe when he got attacked. Diverted and confused, the croc let go of Pascoe's leg and retreated. The victim suffered muscle damage to his left leg, but was found to be in otherwise stable condition when he got to the local hospital.

A year later, Lachlan McGregor, seventeen, was hunting magpie geese at Dhipiri, a remote water hole near the Glyde River in the

Arnhem Land region of the Northern Territory. He made the near-fatal mistake of stepping on the head of a submerged crocodile.

He later told reporters that he and his group were walking back at a leisurely pace. When he stood on the croc's head, it latched onto his leg and pulled him back into the water, but released him after three or four seconds. After that he ran as fast and as far as he could. Witnesses said they thought the 8.5-foot-long croc was a mother protecting her hatchlings. If that was indeed the case, in all likelihood it saved McGregor's life.

Shortly after Russell Harris and Barry Jefferies were killed and Chantal Burnup was attacked, Northern Territory authorities sent a proposal to the federal government that would have allowed twenty-five trophy crocodiles (longer than 13 feet) to be killed on safari hunts each year. Australia rejected the plan. The environment minister said that permitting visitors to blast away at Australia's wildlife would convey an inaccurate idea about the country's pledge to preserve its indigenous fauna. He added that safari hunting, in his opinion, was not consistent with a modern-day approach to animal welfare and responsible management. Moreover, it was highly unlikely that amateur hunters would be able to kill a crocodile from 50 yards away in a humane manner with the first shot.

The government will continue to permit 600 crocs a year to be shot and trapped by experts, to be used for farming, to harvest their hides and meat, or because they pose a real threat to humans.

Another hunter was saved from almost certain death on November 22, 2003, when a forty-year-old woman from the Pirlangimpi Aboriginal district became detached from a group that had been searching for mud mussels on Melville Island in Arnhem Land in the Northern Territory. The woman foolishly tried to traverse a creek at night during a high tide.

She never saw the saltie that sprung up and bit her on the back. She successfully defended herself by whacking the reptile with her bag of mussels. Like Blowers and McGough, she climbed a tree where she remained overnight. The following morning the croc left the area, and its intended victim went on her way, basically none the worse for wear except for a minor wound that was treated at a local hospital.

Trees are often the only way to escape from an attacking salt-water crocodile. Once high enough, a person can usually wait until the croc gives up and goes away. The main issues for someone in a tree are falling asleep, and the risk that rising waters will put the croc within leaping reach.

A certain Ms. Plumwood, an academic from Sydney, decided to go canoeing alone on the ominously named East Alligator River in Kakadu National Park in 1985. Her story of escape and survival ranks among the most miraculous and improbable in the annals of northern Australia croc attacks.

Plumwood ran into what she thought was a floating log. The log was in fact a very large saltie that instantly went after her frail craft, bumping the canoe repeatedly with its bone-hard nose and threatening to tip it over and hurl its occupant into the water. Knowing that if she were to wind up in the river she would face almost certain death, Plumwood sensibly decided to make a dash for the riverbank.

She made it without incident to the bank and managed to climb a tree that easily supported her weight. No doubt she believed she was safe—for a fleeting second. However, that illusion was brutally shattered when the reptile lunged up and out of the water and managed to get ahold of her legs in a grip as strong as a bear trap. Unable to hold on, Plumwood, suffering from deep puncture wounds, was snatched out of the tree in a heartbeat. Once the croc landed back in the water, it did two death rolls. Normally this would have been enough to either render unconscious or outright kill most victims, but Plumwood was no ordinary item of prey.

When the croc released her in order to get a better and final grip, the plucky Plumwood made a second sprint for the same tree she had just been snatched from moments ago. Not to be denied its dinner, the croc lunged again and was able to chomp down and secure its intended victim in its jaws for a second time.

Holding her firmly by her thighs, the croc plunged back into the water, dragging the helpless Plumwood with it. Amazingly, the reptile released her once again in order to get a better grip and administer the fatal coup de grace. Seizing yet another improbable opportunity to escape with her life, Plumwood wisely eschewed the tree and instead hauled her painfully bleeding body up the bank and as far away from the water as possible.

Park rangers found her sometime later in a swamp, bleeding profusely from her injuries. A large part of one of her thighs had been bitten off by the croc and was hanging on by tendons. But Plumwood survived to tell the tale.

Three years later in Kakadu, an attack had an entirely different and infinitely more gruesome outcome. A local man went fishing at the Oenpelli border crossing at the junction of Arnhem Land and Kakadu. It was (and still is) common for native peoples to catch their dinner on the end of a well-baited line. Thinking the fishing was better elsewhere, he was able to wade to the far side of the crossing. There he contentedly cast his lure for several uneventful hours.

He was not alone. Watching him with intense interest was a large saltwater crocodile. In and of itself, this was nothing to get concerned about. Salties are found in great numbers throughout the area, and the sight of one did not necessarily precipitate a horrendous event. Indigenous people get used to crocs. They learn to live with the reptiles and in general, they exercise sound judgment in their presence.

However, the penalty for complacency can be catastrophic.

When he had finished fishing, the man waded back along a causeway in the direction of his parked car. But by this time the water had risen and he inexplicably fell or slipped into deeper, faster-moving water. He started to float downstream. A group of American tourists were sitting and relaxing on the riverbank, watching and wondering if they should intervene and help the man.

Gathering himself up, he regained his footing and scrambled to the riverbank. The Americans were glad they didn't intercede. It was obvious the man was safe. But it was slippery and muddy. The man was encumbered by a fishing net, and, according to witnesses, a beer which he held in his other hand. Everything conspired to slow him down just long enough to enable the submerged croc to explode out of the water.

The croc had already completed his attack run, and he executed the final phase to perfection. Every variable had been considered and factored into the final equation. The croc had maneuvered himself extremely close to the fisherman. Jaws agape, the reptile seized the already doomed man's head with his long, pointy teeth and clamped down as hard as he could.

The fisherman was instantly decapitated. The croc submerged with the head in his jaws and the corpse, spewing blood from a ghastly stump between the shoulders, floated lazily down the river past the Americans. No remains of the fisherman were ever found. It is entirely possible that alcohol impaired the man's judgment and was a contributing factor in his death.

Looking directly into the gullet of a saltwater crocodile is a terrifying experience. A man's head can easily fit into a saltie's mouth. Not many people have been in that predicament and lived to tell the tale.

In Cairns, North Queensland, in December 2004, eighteen-year-old Drew Ramsden was having a few drinks with a group of friends when he went to the lip of the Barron River at a basin named Lake Placid at approximately 10:30 P.M. to wash his face. He knelt down, leaned over, and plunged his head into the water. Unfortunately he was unable to hear his mates as they frantically shouted at him, trying to warn him of the 8-foot-long croc that was stealthily approaching. They threw rocks and beer cans at the reptile, but were unable to deter it from getting closer and closer.

Drew lifted his head out of the water just in time to hear his friends' hysterical warnings; then, he felt the reptile's teeth scraping his skull. When Drew raised his head, it more than likely saved his life. The croc was unable to get a firm grip on him, allowing the extremely lucky beer drinker to escape with only a few minor puncture wounds and teeth marks on his head and chin.

Another river was the scene of a fatal attack in 1985, when Beryl Wruck, forty, attended a party on the banks of the Daintree River, north of Cairns, Queensland. Everyone in the group was from the area, well aware of the crocodiles that lived in the river and the dangers they posed. Perhaps they did not know that the safety net erected to protect the site where they were partying had been removed for repairs, and had not yet been repositioned.

In any case, it was a hot December night, and several members of the group decided to wade into the river to cool off after hours of dancing and drinking. The water was very shallow, only 18 inches deep. Surely there was no danger. A witness who was standing next to Beryl said he was rudely shoved aside as the croc rushed toward its victim. When the saltie took hold of Beryl, it threw her upwards, somersaulting her into the air. There were no screams, only a loud splash as she landed back in the water and the saltie dragged her to certain death.

An ensuing search party looked for a week, but nothing was ever found—no Beryl . . . no croc.

■ ■ ■

Even large, land-based motor vehicles are not exempt from salt-water crocodile attacks. In late January 2006, a croc catapulted itself at a passing four-wheel-drive truck on the Kakadu Highway near Jabiru. The 6.5-foot-long croc had abruptly materialized from a culvert drain and hurtled itself into the path of the truck, which was driven by a local scientist.

The animal died on impact and was given to local Aborigines, who cooked and ate it. It happened so suddenly, the driver hadn't had any time to react and try to avoid the airborne reptile. Croc experts said the animals often move into culvert fishing sites and stay there for the entire wet season because they're attracted to the fish.

Garry Lindner, a crocodile management officer at Kakadu National Park, said the croc was probably startled by the passing vehicle and just leapt in the wrong direction when it heard the vehicle coming.

A police blunder in March 2005 nearly resulted in tragedy. Officers in Kununurra in the far north of Western State responded to an emergency call from a shocked woman who returned home earlier than expected from a holiday and discovered a 6-foot saltwater crocodile in the laundry room of her home.

The saltie had been caught by a friend of her son's, who was a licensed croc catcher. He had intended to take it to a nearby sanctuary the next day and release it. In the meantime, he'd stashed the croc for safekeeping in the mother's home.

Believing the animal to be a relatively harmless freshwater croc, the police took it to Lily Creek Lagoon, a popular swimming hole, and set it free. When they learned of the mistake, alarmed wildlife officials immediately warned all residents, especially children (and including dogs) to avoid the area.

After a massive search that lasted several weeks, the croc was found 28 miles upstream from where it had been released. Attempts to trap and remove the saltie from the lagoon were unsuccessful, leaving officials no choice but to shoot the animal.

The returning vacationer wasn't the only one who got a nasty surprise. Ian White, an employee of the Northern Land Council in Jabiru, was sitting at his desk at home one Sunday in February 2006 when he happened to look out the window at his garden. The sun bounced off something black and gold. Ian thought it was a goanna (a large lizard), but then realized it was a croc. Rangers removed the 6.5-foot-long reptile from Ian's carport and later released it at the South Alligator River boat ramp.

A 3-foot saltie took advantage of one of Darwin's many amenities when it went for a swim in a public swimming pool in Palmerston, south of Darwin, in January 2005. Swimmers were quite alarmed when they realized they were sharing the Olympic-sized pool at the Palmerston Leisure Center with the 3.5-foot-long male reptile.

Police and Parks and Wildlife personnel had no difficulty in getting people to evacuate the pool while they easily captured the animal. The croc was very calm and seemed to be in poor health.

Could the majority of these crocodile attacks have been avoided? The answer is an unqualified yes. Experts agree that simply by using common sense and avoiding too much alcohol when in croc country dramatically reduces the chances of becoming a statistic.

CASH CROCS

Crocodile farming began in Queensland in the 1960s, and later extended into the Northern Territory and to Western Australia. Hides and meat products are derived from both saltwater and freshwater crocodiles. About eleven farms in Australia provide various vendors with crocodiles. Several smaller farms dispense subadult crocodiles to other farms.

About ten farms have the ability to process the crocs, and six are licensed for export.

Legs, bodies, and tails are the main sources of meat, while the teeth, claws, and skulls are used for the tourist souvenir trade. The biggest outlets for crocodile meat are Australian hotels and restaurants, and Chinese and Asian markets, where croc meat is widely used in folk medicinal remedies for influenza and colds.

In 1994 Australia exported 12,849 pounds (5,828 kilograms) of crocodile meat. In 2000 the number increased to 123,426 pounds (55,985 kilograms). In 1998 exports produced U.S. $2,220,000 (Australian $3 million), and in the same year international commerce in all crocodile products generated U.S. $222,200,000 (Australian $300 million) in revenues.

Egg collecting is another source of revenue. Harvesting of wild eggs has little effect on the population due to the high mortality rate of hatchlings. Landowners are typically paid U.S. $3.70 (Australian $5) per egg to conserve nesting habitat.

It has been recognized that crocodiles are important to Australia's tourist industry. Many crocodile parks use monies derived from tourist activities to finance crocodile research.

Crocodile farms are also connected to the tourist industry. Some have croc cruises, photos, feeding shows, and tours of the facilities, all of which generate income and increase public awareness concerning the importance of croc conservation. They present a favorable image to the public, which in turn generates not only interest in crocodiles but also goodwill.

Publicity is also an important factor. The aforementioned Steve Irwin (the Crocodile Hunter) is only one of several conservationists/media stars in Australia. Eco-friendly expeditions and televised exploits present crocs and their plight in a favorable light.

Kakadu National Park generated U.S. $2,116,400 ($A2.86 million) in revenues for 2003–2004. The estimated total visitors (including children under sixteen) was 170,423, and the number of adult paying visitors not including seasonal tickets was 136,571. Commercial permits for the same period include: 100 tour operator permits, 849 camping and bushwalking permits, 21 photography permits, and 27 filming permits.

Crocodiles, especially large man-eaters like the saltie, are draws that attract people to national parks. Tourists and locals want to see crocs in the wild, in their natural habitat. In the past twenty-seven years, only two people have been killed in Kakadu. If you exercise caution, the chances of getting injured or eaten by a croc are extremely slim.

Many people have a ghoulish attraction to places where victims have been killed and attacks have occurred. Reptilian assaults on humans fascinate tourists and draw them in.

CONSERVATION

Like many other species of crocodilians, the major threat facing the freshwater crocodile is habitat destruction. Water diversion for irrigation projects, erosion of nesting sites, and loss of riparian habitat also factor into the equation.

Highly poisonous cane toads have been known to cause the deaths of adults and juveniles in smaller population groups. Small-scale illegal hunting and poaching exists, but it does not greatly impact the total population. The hides of freshwater crocodiles have a low commercial value, making them less vulnerable to commercial exploitation.

In Australia the saltwater crocodile is also faced with habitat loss. Nesting sites in the Northern Territory are being destroyed by feral water buffaloes, which trample traditional areas. On the South Alligator River, anchorage of rafting mats of herbage is being broken down, causing the mats to glide away during the wet season.

There is a high acceptance level for the use of nets to catch barramundi (a large and very tasty fish) far upstream of tidal river mouths, and in many instances, into breeding tracts. Crocodiles can become ensnared in the nets and fishermen can disturb nesting sites.

CHAPTER FOURTEEN

THE CHINESE ALLIGATOR

■ ■ Unlike its American cousin, which is flourishing in its habitat, the Chinese alligator (*Alligator sinensis*) is facing extinction. Along with the Philippine crocodile, it is one of the world's most endangered crocodilians. Also known as the Yangtze alligator, Yow Lung, and T'o, it is confined to tracts around the lower Yangtze River (Jiangsu, Zhejiang, and Anhui).

The majority of wild Chinese alligators live in thirteen small protected areas within a 167.2-square-mile (433 square kilometers) reserve, the Anhui Research Center of Chinese Alligator Reproduction (ARC-CAR) in Anhui province. Experts predict a population increase of around 15 percent per year in protected areas. The habitat consists of small ponds that are situated either within or abutting villages that are completely circumscribed by rice fields, or are borderline water bodies positioned in low hills.

Although the alligator sanctuaries are governed by the Anhui Province Forest Department, the ponds are under direct oversight of the regional villages, which utilize them for an assortment of enterprises, such as duck raising, fish farming, buffalo wallows, and crop irrigation. The wild population—meaning those alligators not in protected areas—is declining at a yearly rate of between 4 and 6 percent.

Adults rarely weigh more than 97 pounds (44 kilograms), and max out at around 6.5 feet (2 meters), making this one of the smaller crocodilians. Preferred habitat for this secretive species includes low-elevation agricultural and tree-farm communes of up to 328 feet (100 meters) above sea level, slow-moving freshwater rivers and streams, as well as lakes, ponds, and swamps. Because they live at relatively northern latitudes, they spend between six and seven months a year hibernating in intricate burrow structures in order to avoid the cold. In May they emerge from their dens to bask, and in June, as the temperatures rise, they begin to make nocturnal sorties in search of food.

The Chinese alligator feeds on aquatic invertebrates such as snails and mussels, for which their teeth are adapted, and vertebrates such as fish. Like all crocodilians they are opportunistic hunters, and will also eat ducks and rats when they are available.

The estimated wild population is under 200, and possibly as few as 50. The IUCN classifies the Chinese alligator as "Critically Endangered." The biggest problem facing the Chinese alligator is habitat destruction related to profound human population stresses.

Most of the alligators are located in modified wetlands adjunct to agricultural tracts (which were altered from marshland to accommodate the growing human population) or tree-farm communes where they are susceptible to human predation.

Notwithstanding legal protection under the Law of Wildlife Conservation of the People's Republic of China, individuals are often killed out of fear (despite their historical association with the mythical Chinese dragon), or because of the difficulties they generate for farmers. Adult Chinese alligators will gladly eat tame ducks, and the alligator's burrows cause drainage problems in fields.

In local markets many of their organs are sold as cures for a variety of ailments. The animals may also be gathered for sale to zoos or government-supported farms.

Because of osteoderms on the ventral scales, the hides of this species are difficult to tan, and they have little commercial value in international markets.

Captive breeding programs have been successful in China. The Bronx Zoo in New York, the St. Augustine Alligator Farm in Florida, and the Rockefeller Refuge in Texas also maintain captive breeding programs. Currently there are around 200 Chinese alligators in zoos outside China (approximately 150 in fourteen U.S. zoos, and seven in four European zoos).

Earnings from the licit export of Chinese alligators are needed to bolster the continuing prosperity of captive breeding programs and conservation. The historically negative perceptions of local people who live within close proximity to the alligators are slowly changing. Where before they regarded the animals merely as harmful pests to be exterminated (whenever and wherever feasible), now they realize that conservation of alligators is important.

It is highly unlikely that a Chinese alligator ever attacked anyone.

CHAPTER FIFTEEN

THE FUTURE OF HUMAN/ CROCODILIAN RELATIONS

■ ■ It is always a risky business to look into the future to try to predict what will or will not happen. Prognostications are often a product of wishful thinking and a manifestation of a subliminal desire to impose a particular set of values and ethos upon other people. Judgments, even those based on computer-generated projections, are not infallible by any means. They are only as good as the data fed into them and the capacity of the computers to process the data. Moreover data and the anticipated projections can always be manipulated and subsequently skewed to represent a desired point of view or outcome.

Crocodilians have been on the earth for over 200 million years and have changed little during that time. They have survived cataclysmic changes that have devastated and wreaked havoc on other species. The crocodilian design structure is perfectly suited for the particular environments in which the animals invariably thrive. Over millennia these habitats have changed little. All crocodilians are marine reptiles, whether they live in salt- or freshwater, and although much of their habitat is similar, each particular domain has its peculiarities and specific demands it makes on the crocodilians that inhabit them.

Although they are hardy and resilient animals, they are, by virtue of physiological characteristics and requirements, confined to warmer, more temperate latitudes. Nevertheless they are found throughout the world, sometimes in great numbers and profusion.

All crocodilians (alligators, caiman, crocodiles, and gharials) are keystone species. They are the megapredators of their ecosystems. The health of specific crocodilian populations within a given ecosystem invariably reflects the general vigor and vitality of that particular ecosystem. In this regard all crocodilians play a vital and important role in maintaining the integrity and vitality of ecosystems scattered throughout much of the world.

When alligator populations crash in Florida or Louisiana, it has the same deleterious effect as crocodile populations declining in Africa, gharial numbers dwindling in India, or caiman populations decreasing in Central or South America. They are, if you will, living barometers. By monitoring the behavior of crocodilians as it relates to breeding, mortality rates, and average weights within a given area—typically consisting of two or three and up to several hundred square miles or square kilometers—biologists, herpetologists, and other scientists can accurately extrapolate their findings to encompass a much larger expanse. From these findings, scientists can make accurate measurements and judgments concerning the health of the entire ecosystem and all of the other resident avian, reptilian, and mammalian inhabitants.

Like all other animals (including humans), crocodilians require a certain amount of space in order to thrive and even survive. The more space they have, the healthier individual populations are as a whole. When unnaturally crowded together, they are collectively and individually stressed. Alligators, caiman, crocodiles, and gharials are highly individualistic, although they tolerate each other's presence within the restrictions of well-defined parameters such as size, available territory, and gender.

They are not herd animals like ungulates, nor do they form tightly knit familial or matriarchal-led groups or clans like elephants or lemurs.

With a few exceptions, all crocodilians tend to be large, heavy animals and when they attack humans the wounds they inflict are horrific. Powerful jaw muscles combine with, on average, seventy cone-shaped, sharply pointed teeth specifically designed to tear and puncture while removing large chunks of flesh as quickly and expeditiously as possible. They are extremely adept at concealment both above and below the surface of water and are capable of attacking with speeds that belie their size.

While such programs are obviously well-intended, it is difficult if not impossible to measure the effectiveness of public education and awareness programs on municipal and state levels that earnestly attempt to make people aware of the inherent dangers associated with either inadvertent or deliberate contact with crocodilians. There is little or no empirical or anecdotal evidence that suggests such warnings and conspicuously posted signs have any demonstrable effect on the number of attacks on people by alligators, caiman, and crocodiles.

In many instances, alcohol abuse is a contributing factor in alligator, caiman, and crocodile attacks that result in death or serious injury. Human error and lack of sound judgment also play a major role in putting people at grave personal risk. It is not against the law to act in stupid or foolish ways, and common sense cannot be legislated. Luck, whether it be good or bad, frequently determines whether a person escapes unscathed, is eaten alive, or suffers horrible, disfiguring wounds that invariably require lengthy and expensive periods of recuperation.

Tourists, campers, and hikers are venturing into crocodilian habitat throughout the world in increasing numbers, and this in turn also dramatically expands the probabilities for human/crocodilian conflict.

Increased tourism generates large sums of additional monies for individual municipalities' and states' coffers in the form of air, land, or rail transportation to and from specific crocodilian habitats, local taxes and other financial levies, hotel and motel rooms, automobile rentals, and national park and recreation area fees. Additionally, taxed supplies and sundry items that visitors usually purchase such as gasoline, clothing, food, film, beverages, and souvenirs contribute significantly to the economies of local, smaller communities whose residents are often heavily dependent on tourism for a large part of their income. There is money to be made from crocodiles and alligators, and many people have demonstrated they will travel great distances and spend considerable amounts of currency to see crocodilians in their native habitats.

Tourism and the often much-needed revenue associated with the industry are often successfully coupled with crocodile conservation programs. This is especially true in parts of rural Africa, where impoverished people throughout the continent are starting to understand the connection between crocodilian species and hard cash in the form of Western currency. The reptiles are increasingly being regarded and recognized as natural resources that can be profitably husbanded and managed. On the other hand, nonfatal attacks invariably strain the resources of many cash-strapped municipalities. Doctors and hospitals are frequently forced to absorb the cost of complicated, extensive, expensive, and lengthy courses of medical treatment and rehabilitation.

Typically underfunded, undermanned, and overworked local emergency services in the form of land-based ambulances, airborne medevac helicopters, and sometimes marine resources are financially strained due to the increasing number of time-consuming rescue operations they are obliged to initiate and complete. Many hospitals situated near crocodilian habitat that attracts increasingly large numbers of tourists are small, somewhat isolated medical facilities whose primary mission is to serve the basic needs of local populations. In many instances they are ill equipped or staffed to adequately care for victims of crocodile attacks and are capable of rendering only rudimentary emergency treatment. Casualties of crocodilian assaults often have to be transported at public expense over great distances to larger hospitals where more complete and thorough treatment can be administered.

In cases where attacks result in fatalities, reasonable and realistic efforts are made to recover bodies or remains and return them to the next of kin. These operations also involve a combination of land, air, and marine resources the considerable cost of which is absorbed by the state.

As human populations continue to grow unchecked throughout the world and persist in infringing upon crocodilian habitat, crocodilian/human conflicts will increase exponentially. Loss of habitat is arguably the greatest threat to crocodilian populations wherever they exist in the world.

Appropriation of crocodilian habitat for agricultural, hydroelectric, or fishing industries by burgeoning numbers of people in Africa and India will continue to infringe and negatively affect the general health and well-being of crocodilian populations. Crocodiles often compete with indigenous people for food and income sources, usually fish, creating an adversarial relationship that is rarely resolved to the mutual satisfaction of reptile and human.

It matters little to the specific crocodilian inhabitants if the reason for their loss of available territory and associated food resources is due to western expansion of Miami-Dade County into the Everglades of Florida or the increasing numbers of African villagers who must catch more fish yearly in order to survive. In either case, humans severely compromise crocodilian food resources and crowd crocodilians into smaller and smaller available territories and increase the potential for human/crocodilian conflict.

In the massive and overpopulated subcontinent of India, loss of crocodilian habitat is also increasing for much the same reasons. Preservation efforts are also expanding. International organizations such as CITIES, IUCN, the Crocodile Specialist Group and others too numerous to mention are adding their expertise, financial clout, lobbying, and organizational skills and their collective ability to create positive dialogues between often disparate and competing interests on local, state or province, national, and international levels to create and foster not only understanding but also tangible gains for both crocodiles and the millions of people that share their habitat.

With some exceptions, most crocodilian populations in the world are healthy. Several species are thriving and a few are in danger of becoming extinct. Captive breeding programs and sustainable management proce-dures are being initiated in many parts of the world where crocodilian populations have already declined or are in danger of declining. In many instances human intervention has proved to be an extremely successful and effective tool in preserving crocodiles and their dwindling habitat.

Despite more stringent regulations and enforcement procedures on municipal and governmental levels, crocodilians will no doubt continue to be exploited for their meat and hides. Impoverished people through-out the world will circumvent local and state laws. Black marketeers will abet these practices and in some instances make a detrimental contribu-tion to the general health and well-being of specific species.

A relatively sizeable number of misinformed and misguided individ-uals will continue to be attracted to hatchling alligators and caiman. When purchasing these animals as pets, they support and encourage the illegal pet trade which will no doubt continue to flourish. Invariably these reptiles quickly grow to an unmanageable size. When they are re-leased by their owners in public lakes or any other body of freshwater, innocent people are put at grave risk, as are the local authorities who must either capture or cull the reptiles.

Nevertheless, the future is guardedly bright for crocodilians in gen-eral. A successful confluence of a myriad of viable conservation strate-gies, increased public awareness and appreciation, and the improvement in the daily lives and future of impoverished peoples throughout the world who have been empowered to equate crocodilians with long term enrichment leaves little room for pessimism.

Hopefully all crocodilians will continue to survive and flourish for the next 200 million years.

INDEX

10